MARACATU FOR DRUMSET AND PERCUSSION

A Guide to the Traditional Brazilian Rhythms of Maracatu de Baque Virado

By Scott Kettner

with Aaron Shafer-Haiss and Michele Nascimento

ISBN 978-1-4584-1773-2

HAL•LEONARD®
CORPORATION

7777 W. BLUEMOUND RD. P.O. BOX 13819 MILWAUKEE, WI 53213

In Australia Contact:
Hal Leonard Australia Pty. Ltd.
4 Lentara Court
Cheltenham, Victoria, 3192 Australia
Email: ausadmin@halleonard.com.au

Visit Hal Leonard Online at
www.halleonard.com

Edited by Rick Mattingly
Cover Design by Lula Marcondes
Photos by Jason Gardner unless otherwise noted
Music Transcription by Scott Kettner and Aaron Shafer-Haiss
Historical research by Scott Kettner and Michele Nascimento
Historical text by Michele Nascimento
Translations by Michele Nascimento and Scott Kettner

Audio Tracks recorded at The Soap Box Factory, Brooklyn, NY
Engineered by Scott Kettner and Aaron Shafer-Haiss
Assistant Engineer Pat Noonan
Mixed and Mastered by Scott Anderson
All tracks were performed by Scott Kettner and Aaron Shafer-Haiss except:

Track 9: "Estrela Brilhante é Um Brilho" (public domain): performed by Estrela
Brilhante and Nation Beat featuring Mestre Walter on vocals, Jorge Martins,
Walter S. Filho, Walcyr S. de França, Marcelo Tompson, Cláudio Torô,
Eduardo Guedes, and Scott Kettner on percussion.

Track 59: "Baque de Brooklyn" (written by Scott Kettner): performed by
Maracatu New York with Aaron Shafer-Haiss, Jeff Duneman, and Scott
Kettner on percussion.

Track 98: "Temos Rei, Temos Rainha" (public domain) performed by Maracatu New York with Liliana Araújo on vocals and Jorge Martins on percussion.

This book is dedicated to Mestre Walter, Dona Marivalda, Walter de França Filho, Jorge Martins and Billy Hart for sharing their music and culture with me. Without their support none of this material would be presented here.

After a performance, members of Estrela Brilhante carry their drums through the dimly lit streets on their way home. Alto Zé do Pinho, Recife, 2004.

Table of Contents

iNTRODUCTiON

My goal in writing this book is to present an accessible and pragmatic approach to learning and understanding the instruments and basic rhythms of Maracatu de Baque Virado and how to approach these rhythms on the drumset. It's important for me to point out that this is just an overview, and even though I have spent many years studying, teaching, playing, and performing maracatu in Recife and throughout the world, there's a lot I'm still learning and a lot that is not presented here. The traditional maracatu groups are always coming up with new ideas, arrangements, and new variations on their music; therefore, it's impossible to write a single book that embodies a rhythm and culture as rich as maracatu. However, I have tried to present the foundation to help you develop a vocabulary that will enhance your understanding of the rhythms, melodies, and culture of Maracatu de Baque Virado.

I also took great care to pay respect and give credit to all of the traditional maracatu nations in Recife, Pernambuco that I have referred to in this book, and I hope you do the same when learning and sharing this material. Maracatu is not just a rhythm, it's a culture and a way of life. The musicians, dancers, and administrators of traditional maracatu groups dedicate their entire lives to this culture. This is not something they do as a hobby; for maracatuzeiros, playing maracatu is a way of life that helps maintain a certain social structure within their communities. When studying the music in this book you should always remember that the little black dots on the page don't mean anything without the culture and the people who make up this tradition. This book is just a peek into a fraction of what a traditional maracatu group does.

In the following pages I'll share some of the rhythms and baques (beats) that I've learned from my mentors and teachers in Recife over the past decade of researching. I'll also share my own interpretations and variations that have evolved over the years of playing this music.

I hope that the material in this book will help deepen your understanding of maracatu and inspire you to further explore and study this music and culture. Remember that this is just a guide to help get you started. There's no better way to learn a style of music than going to the source and drinking from the fountain. So when the spirit moves you, go to Recife and learn with the traditional maracatu nations!

Remember to have fun and keep an open mind while studying this material.

Scott Kettner

ACKNOWLEDGEMENTS

I'd like to thank the following people for inspiring me, teaching me and encouraging me:

Michele Nascimento-Kettner, Billy Hart, Jim Lynch, Mr. Sanders, Larry Crook, Rick Shiley, Skye Steele, Eduardo Guedes, Mike Savino, Mike Lavalle, Liliana Araújo, Nanny Assis, Raphael McGregor, Rob Curto, Aaron Shafer-Haiss, Patti Sullivan, Jill Harris, everyone from Corpos Percussivos, Drica Souza, Memo Acevedo, Steve Nigohosian and the entire LP family, Joe Testa, Ben Davies, Mark Wessels, and the Vic Firth family, Aaron Vishria, Terry Bissette and the TAMA family, Paul Cellucci and the entire Sabian family, Cyro Baptista, Cabelo, Mom and Dad, Peter Karl, Bola, Carlinhos Pandeiro de Ouro, Jorge Martins, David Greeley, Frank London, Jeff Duneman, Josh Dekaney, Lula Marcondes, Mona Kayhan, Phil Ballman, Tom Frouge, Stanton Moore, Robert Schoville, Tony DiSanza, Tim & Pat O'Keefe, Bola, Bobby Sanabria, Jamey Haddad, everyone from Maracatu New York and every musician, teacher and friend who has helped lift me to the next level.

And a special thanks to these folks for playing an important role in this book:

Ed Uribe, Michael Spiro, Stanton Moore, AMAMPE, Walter de França Filho (Waltinho), Mestre Ivaldo, Mestre Walter, Mestre Shacon, Presidente Fabio, Mestre Hugo, Itaiguara, Maureliano, Fábrica Estudios, Jeff Moura, Pablo Lopes, Malu Donanzan.

A very special thanks to Dona Marivalda, Mestre Walter and the entire community of Maracatu Nação Estrela Brilhante.

—Scott Kettner

ABOUT THE AUTHORS

Picture by Petr Cancura

When **Scott Kettner** looks at a map, he sees a direct line that connects the rivers of northeastern Brazil to the parishes of New Orleans and the streets of Brooklyn. A master percussionist, bandleader, producer, and songwriter, Kettner is the guiding force behind Nation Beat, a band whose teeming, vibrant rhythms find common ground in the primal maracatu rhythm of Brazil's northeastern region, the Big Easy's funky, hypnotic second-line and strolling Mardi Gras Indians, and the unfettered freedom of big-city downtown jazz.

For Kettner, the discovery of maracatu, an Afro-Brazilian rhythm from the northeast of Brazil, was a life-changing experience. The great jazz drummer Billy Hart, who served as Kettner's instructor at New York's New School University, first informed him of this music. Intrigued by this rhythm, Kettner decided to move to Brazil and learn more about maracatu and other styles of music from northeastern Brazil. Upon graduating in 2000, he spent a year living in the country, based primarily in the northeastern city of Recife, studying the music and culture of maracatu and other, even more obscure Brazilian rhythms with his new mentor, Jorge Martins.

After returning to the States in 2002, Kettner assembled Nation Beat, incorporating the maracatu rhythms with elements of jazz and the myriad sounds of Louisiana. The similarities between the Brazilian music he came to love and the southern rhythms he grew up with became apparent to Kettner as he began writing for the new band. But Kettner was never content only to record the music with his own group. At the same time he returned from Brazil to play maracatu, he also launched a school in Brooklyn, Maracatu New York, in order to alert others to what he'd learned. Still going strong today, the institution is described as "New York's first and only maracatu ensemble dedicated to the performance and knowledge" of the music and culture. Maracatu New York is also the first organized maracatu group in the USA. Since bringing maracatu to the States, maracatu—due largely to Kettner's efforts—has begun to find a foothold in the USA, and there are now many groups all over the country beginning to play this unique rhythm and music from Brazil.

When he's not on the road touring with Nation Beat or one of his other groups, you can often find Kettner in his Brooklyn studio teaching drumset and percussion and writing songs for and producing other artists.

For more information, visit **www.scottkettner.com**

Aaron Shafer-Haiss is a graduate of Interlochen Arts Academy and The New School for Jazz and Contemporary Music, and was introduced to maracatu after meeting Scott Kettner in 2004. After a few years of studying the music of Northeast Brazil in New York, Aaron made his first visit to Recife in 2008 where he lived for six months with percussionist Jorge Martins (Estrela Brilhante do Recife, Cascabulho) and studied with percussion masters Guga Santos (Mestre Galo Preto, Dona Cila do Coco), and Mestre Nana (Escola de Samba Galeria do Ritmo), among others. In addition to an in-depth study of all the regional music he could come across, Aaron was fortunate enough to be able to attend ensaios (rehearsals) with traditional maracatus Estrela Brilhante do Recife, Nação Porto Rico, and Leão Coroado. Aaron is Project Co-Director for Maracatu New York and plays LP Percussion instruments and Vic Firth sticks exclusively.

Michele Nascimento is a Ph.D. candidate writing her dissertation on Transnational Regionalism in Latin America. She is a researcher of the literature and culture of Latin America and, first and foremost, a literary scholar who believes in interdisciplinary dialogues. Nascimento is originally from Pernambuco, Brazil, and was raised in the North Zone of Recife, the cradle of the most diverse folkloric rhythms of the state of Pernambuco. For Nascimento, researching about maracatu and its rich and diverse groups has been part of both an insightful and rewarding intellectual/personal journey.

AUTHORS' NOTE

Throughout this book we'll take a look at some of the different baques (beats) used by some of the traditional maracatu groups in Recife. Each nação (nation/group) has their own unique way of playing these rhythms. Try to find online videos and recordings of the groups mentioned throughout this book and examine their swing feels, tempos, sticking patterns, and arrangements. Maracatu de Baque Virado, like any style of music, is a language and is constantly evolving and changing. You have to listen closely over and over again to begin to understand the different accents and ways of articulation. Also, always keep in mind that this music is communal and has been passed down orally for centuries, which means that a lot of the information is in a constant flux, and what is played today will most likely be different as time goes on. Try to get a few of your friends together to play through the material in this book. Practice switching instruments and making up your own arrangements. You never know, but this could end up being a seed for your own local maracatu percussion group and inspire you to travel to Recife and learn with the maracatu masters.

While conducting research for this book we were very fortunate to have had the chance to interview and take lessons with a handful of the best maracatu masters in Recife. During these lessons I realized how much maracatu has changed since I started studying it in 1999. This presented a huge obstacle for my partners and I. How do we write a book about a style of music that is constantly evolving and changing and also contradicting itself? We structured this book simply as a snapshot of the groups interviewed for this book at the time we were in Recife. A lot of the material also comes from my notes and lessons that I had while I was living in Recife in 2001–2002. We have done our best to present you with an honest representation of the rhythms, music, and culture of maracatu. Many of the elements in this book are timeless and will remain a part of maracatu forever, while some of the elements will evolve over time and morph into new manifestations. We hope you enjoy this snapshot of Maracatu de Baque Virado as much as we enjoyed assembling it for you.

BACKGROUND

Traditional Maracatu Nations vs. Percussion Groups

Before getting deep into this book it's very important for you to understand and know the difference between a traditional maracatu nation and a percussion group that plays maracatu rhythms. A maracatu nation is deeply rooted to the Candomblé religion and maintains their religious obligations on a daily basis. These nations always have a calunga doll(s) and an entire court of dancers, they socially interact with their local community, they are made up mostly of African descendant Brazilians, and they are tied to a tradition dating back to slavery in Brazil. These are only a few characteristics of a traditional maracatu nation. The music, songs and rhythms make up only a small part of a traditional maracatu nation. On the other hand, a percussion group who plays maracatu rhythms is not considered a traditional maracatu nation. A few examples of percussion groups from around the world who play maracatu but are not a traditional maracatu nation are Maracatu Nação Pernambuco, Rio Maracatu, Maracatu New York, Maracatu Estrela do Norte, Maracatu Nação Maracambuco, Baque Mulher, Corpos Percussivos, and many more.

While having a conversation with Dona Marivalda (Queen/President of Estrela Brilhante) during an interview in 2011, she expressed frustration towards the percussion groups around the world who play maracatu: "No one ever brings me or the traditional maracatus to travel and tour because there's so many maracatu groups springing up all over the world now. Who needs us?" I was very quick to correct her and explained that these percussion groups will never be equal to a traditional maracatu nation, and that these groups are breeding more interest in the traditional maracatu nations. Try to remember this story as you begin your journey in learning maracatu. Always remember that this is music that plays an important role in their community. When you have a chance, go to Recife and give something back in return for all of the rich music and culture that is being shared in this book. It could be as simple as buying their CD instead of copying it.

Use of the Word "Tradition" in This Book

I always take great caution when using the word "tradition," especially when referring to a living art form that is always changing and evolving, like maracatu. Most people use the word "tradition" in a context to refer to something that hasn't changed or evolved over time, whereas the word itself simply implies something that has been passed down from past generations. Some of the important "traditional" maracatu masters that I interviewed for this book make a strong effort to change their grooves and songs each year to be more contemporary and stand out from other groups as much as possible, while still maintaining a discourse of being "traditional." Moreover, each group I interviewed for this book had a completely different story as to what their idea of the traditional maracatu rhythms, history, and religion are. Therefore, my conclusion is that each maracatu nation is a microcosm living its own unique tradition, which is in constant flux and always evolving and making new rules.

Parallel with the music, there are the rituals and ceremonies of the Candomblé and Jurema religions, which have taken place for generations and to this day maintain a strong presence and influence over the maracatu groups. The religion and the ceremonies that take place in these groups are what sets the "traditional" maracatu groups apart from the percussion groups who play maracatu rhythms. Although members of traditional maracatu groups are not required to participate in the religious aspects of this manifestation, religion is always present when a member of a group speaks about or performs maracatu.

In this book the word "tradition" will always refer to the maracatu groups who are deeply linked to these religious ceremonies and have a strong commitment to their African ancestors but nevertheless are constantly creating new ideas and new traditions.

Dispelling the Agogô Bell in Maracatu

This is another element that helps determine the difference between a traditional maracatu group and a percussion group that plays maracatu. As of today, you will never hear the agogô bell being played in a traditional maracatu group. The belief is that during research for his book *Maracatus do Recife*, Guerra Peixe transcribed a rhythmic cell from the onguê bell and applied it to the agogô bell in his transcriptions. In the 1990s, Nação Pernambuco recorded the first maracatu CD and used an agogô bell, since it was more accessible and had more commercial appeal at the time. Because of the popularity of Peixe's book and Pernambuco's CD, many people around the world adopted this and considered it as a traditional maracatu instrument. To make things even more complicated, Mestre Luiz da França and Mestre Afonso from Nação Leão Coroado call the onguê (a single bell instrument) an agogô bell (a double bell instrument). This also could have led to the confusion in Peixe's book. So keep in mind that while it is perfectly okay to play an agogô bell in your group, you won't hear it being played in a traditional maracatu nation.

Swing Feel

This always seems to be the main topic of conversation when we talk about a style of music that is foreign to our ears. Every culture and every style of music throughout the world has its own unique swing feel, or accent, as I like to refer to it. This is one of the main characteristics that helps define a style of music, like a dialect or accent helps define the region of a country where a person comes from. Maracatu has a very strong lilt, and to make things even more interesting each group plays with varying degrees of this lilt. There's no way to explain this swing feel with words. You have to listen to the music until you internalize it. I've done my best to provide you with examples on the CD, which should help you begin to hear this swing feel. Try playing along and singing the caixa parts to begin capturing that feel. Also, search for videos online of the groups mentioned in this book to help you dig even deeper into that swing feel. You could also refer to my good friend Michael Spiro's book *The Conga Drummer's Guidebook*. He has a section that breaks down the Brazilian swing feel nicely.

Loas/Toadas

Another thing to keep in mind while studying the material in this book is the songs (loas/toadas) of maracatu. Due to the nature of this book we are not exploring the harmonic and melodic aspect of Maracatu de Baque Virado. It's very important that you seek out the traditional songs on your own. This will help you develop a holistic understanding of this music. Without the songs, the rhythms in this book would simply not exist.

Instruments of Maracatu de Baque Virado

This is a list of instruments used in Maracatu de Baque Virado. It's very important to make clear that traditional maracatu nations do not use every instrument listed below; rather, each nation uses a unique combination of instruments that has either a historical, religious, or symbolic purpose within that maracatu nation.

Gonguê – very large, oversized cowbell. The onguê acts as the glue, playing a repetitive "clave" pattern and variations. There is usually only one onguê player in an entire maracatu nation; however, some groups use two or three.

Mineiro (also known as **Ganzá**) – the mineiro or ganzá is a long metal tube filled with tiny stones or beans and used as a large shaker.

Caixa (also known as **Caixa de Guerra**) – snare drum, made of metal or wood. The caixa is very similar in size to a regular 14-inch snare drum found on a drumset.

Tarol – a shallow snare drum, similar to a piccolo snare, which plays a unique function depending on the maracatu group. The tarol is not found in all maracatu groups.

Apito (**whistle**) – The mestre's whistle functions as an instrument that plays a very important role in the direction of the drum section. The mestre uses the whistle to conduct breaks and signal changes in an arrangement.

Tambor (also known as **Afaia**, **Bombo**, or **Alfaia**) – the large bass drum in maracatu. The tambores were traditionally made from barrels or any material that the slaves could find to make a drum. More recently traditional maracatu groups have started using a

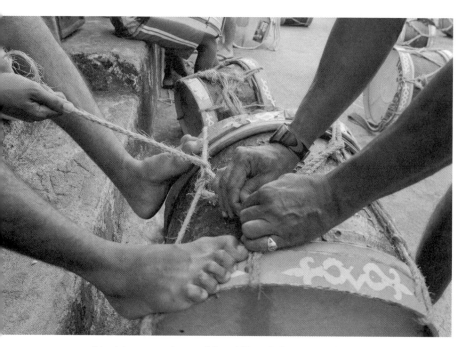

Musicians use the traditional "Cordão" method of rope tuning. Pulling the rope tightens the tension between the wood hoops and the goatskin. Alto Zé do Pinho, 2004.

Mestre Hugo Leonardo of Maracatu Nação Leão da Campina playing the Atabaques in the Terreiro, demonstrating the relationship between Candomblé and maracatu. Photo by Scott Kettner.

hollowed out tree trunk called Macaíba or a cheaper wood called hardboard. Some traditional maracatu groups have three different size alfaias that each serve a specific musical role, which we'll look at as we get into the music section on this book.

Atabaque — The atabaque is a hand drum very similar to a conga that is used during the Candomblé ceremonies. At the time this book was written, Nação Porto Rico is the only group who uses this instrument. In an interview, Nação Aurora Africana mentioned to me that they use this instrument on one song but they have not fully committed to using it yet.

Agbê (also known as **shekere**) — a hollowed out gourd with a beaded skirt fit around it. This instrument is found in many different regions of the world. The agbê is an instrument currently being disputed between some of the mestres and academics in Recife. Mestre Ivaldo (Nação Cambinda Estrela) argues that the agbê was never a traditional instrument of maracatu and that it was used only in Ijexá or Afoxê music, while Mestre Walter (Nação Estrela Brilhante) and Mestre Shacon (Nação Porto Rico) dispute this. They justify the use of an agbê in maracatu because of its use in Candomblé, and since maracatu is rooted in this religion they consider it a legitimate addition to their maracatu nations.

The tambores seem to bring up yet another debate. Few maracatuzeiros (people who play maracatu) agree on a name, spelling, or even the division of this instrument. Mestre Ivaldo argues that the tambores don't have a division of three parts and never did. However Mestre Walter, Mestre Shacon, Mestre Fabio, and Mestre Itaiguara expressed deeply that this division has been a part of their maracatu since the beginning and that this division plays a very important musical role within the melodic conversation between the tambores. In my interview, Mestre Walter described how he places his "tambores mestres" (largest alfaias) on the outside of each line and builds towards the center, with each drum getting smaller. He used the analogy of how a European classical orchestra is constructed, and that the placement of each instrument affects the overall sonic experience the listener and the musician experiences.

Mestre Shacon divides his tambores into three sections with a fourth drum being the improviser. Inspired by the drums used in Candomblé, Shacon created a musical language in Maracatu Porto Rico that is very unique to this group. He divides his alfias using the names of the atabaques (hand drums) used in Candomblé: Melê (largest drum), Yan (middle drum), Biancó (high pitched drum), and the Yandarrum, which is a sacred drum that only someone from the religion can play. This drum is the improviser and does not have a specific rhythm that is played consistently.

Even the name of this drum is undefined. Is it an alfaia, afaia, tambor or a bombo? The drum maker Maureliano (Barravento) had an interesting comment about this. "If it was an alfaia, why don't they call Noite dos Tambores Silenciosos Noite dos Alfaias Silenciosos?" What I realized is that most of the older maracatuzeiros and maracatuzeiras call the bass drums bombo or tambor, while most of the younger generation calls them alfaias. For the sake of keeping things simple for this book I've decided to consistently label it as an alfaia for every example. This is the most universally used term for the drum and will be understood by anyone in Recife or any other part of the world. But it's definitely worth knowing that this drum also has two other names.

The Mystical Journey from Brazil to the USA

Anyone who does research on Maracatu de Baque Virado will ultimately come across the name Katarina Real. She was an American anthropologist who lived in Brazil for many years researching the music and culture of Recife and Pernambuco during the 1960s. She was one of the first foreigners who did research on maracatu and wrote about it at a time when bossa nova and samba were the only styles of music people knew of when they thought about Brazil. Her research, photos, and unique story and travels are known by academics, ethnomusicologists, and anthropologists around the world. But more importantly, her connection and passion to Maracatu de Baque Virado indirectly helped set the stage for this rhythm and culture to come to life in the United States.

Unfortunately, I never had the chance to meet her in person before she passed on, but I was lucky enough to have a few conversations with her by phone, where she shared many of her experiences of living in Recife. The following story was printed in a pamphlet in Portuguese for a ceremony conducted by the Museu do Homem do Nordeste in March 1996. She sent me this pamphlet after one of our discussions, and upon reading this story I was overwhelmed. Maracatu has had a presence in the USA since 1968 thanks to Katarina. Furthermore, Estrela Brilhante, the group that I had become a member of, believed that the Calunga Joventina held the mystical powers for their maracatu group. Calunga Joventina was brought to the US by Katarina, where it lived for almost thirty years. This is the same group that I had become a member of, and I was studying all of their rhythms together with my mentor, Jorge Martins. Was it a coincidence that I was drawn to the rhythms and songs of the same maracatu group that had a presence in the USA for thirty years or was there a deeper reason why I felt a connection to Nação Estrela Brilhante? I certainly can't answer this question, but I do believe in the mystical powers that Joventina and other maracatu calungas carry, and I think the following story will help you understand the significance of Katarina Real's and Joventina's journey to the USA.

"Dona Joventina," Calunga of a Maracatu Nation

Greeting to the authorities,

Distinguished directors and presidents of the groups that belong to the Federação Carnavalesca Pernambucana, FCP (Carnival Federation of Pernambuco) present in the room.

Dearest Queens and Damas de Paço of the Maracatu nations: Estrela Brilhante, Elefante, Porto Rico, Encanto do Pina.

My *compadre*, Mestre Luiz de França, from Leão Coroado. The Honorable Calungas, Mr. Batuqueiros from Nações Encanto do Pina and Elefante and the very dear, old and new, friends that are honoring me with your presence.

Ladies and gentlemen,

In order to avoid me getting nervous, I will invite "Dona Joventina" to speak in my behalf because she is comfortable facing big audiences and she is not afraid of anything. "Dona Joventina, would you like to speak to all of these friendly people now? Then, you now have the floor!"

I am Calunga Dona Joventina, from the old Maracatu Nação Estrela Brilhante, founded in Recife in 1910. I "was born," or if you may prefer, I was carved from noble wood by a very talented *santeiro* (religious leader), whose name is unknown, just before 1910—in other words, I am almost a hundred years old.

I have jointed arms that I can move in any position; I am a complete woman with beautiful breasts and some other things…!!! For many years, Katarina thought that I was pregnant because I have a potbelly, but recently when Dona Regina from this museum examined me naked without my cute clothes she didn't think I was pregnant—she thought that my little belly was typical of a strong African woman, well nourished.

I am mounted on a pedestal, or rather, on a very old fruit bowl; my old fashioned sandals are tied to me with two screws and they are a little loose so I can sway swiftly to the rhythm of maracatu de baque virado. This fruit bowl is similar to those ones used by the women that belonged to the sisterhood of Our Lady of the Rosary of Black Men. Some centuries ago these women went from door to door right before the festivities of Our Lady of the Rosary with their bowls to collect food and money for the festival.

For many decades, I paraded during Carnival and danced in the hands of many damas de paço always receiving acclamation and admiration from the Pernambucan people. But it was only in 1961 that I got to know the anthropologist Katarina Real when she came to the Nação Estrela Brilhante headquarters. At that time the headquarters was located in the neighborhood of Campo Grande, here in Recife. Katarina went there to interview Dona Assunção, that, at that time, was the president of the association and also the widow of Estrela Brilhante's founder.

The adoptive child of Dona Assunção was Lenira, a very beautiful and friendly teenager. She was the *dama do paço* that carried me to dance and play during the carnival parades. I can tell you that Lenira was an extraordinary, wonderful dama do paço and I was always happy when I danced and spun with her.

Every time Katarina arrived at the headquarters of Estrela Brilhante to talk to Dona Assunção she asked Lenira to bring me from the room hidden in the back of the house where I used to be kept and that Katarina never got to enter. Then, Katarina asked Lenira to dance with me because she thought I was very beautiful and mysterious. I started to like this foreigner that had such a strange accent.

Estrela Brilhante paraded in the carnivals of 1961 through 1964, despite the increasing difficulties that each year brought. There were serious problems and dissenting opinions in the group and every year Dona Assunção had more difficulties organizing the group to parade. In 1964, with much sadness the old Estrela Brilhante performed for the last time in the carnival parades on Conde da Boa Vista Avenue. I think that it was the first and only time this avenue was like a catwalk for popular carnival groups.

I did not see Katarina for a while but I know that she fought to prevent Estrela Brilhante from coming to an end. One day, in 1966, exactly 30 years ago, Dona Assunção wrapped me in at towel and took me to Katarina's apartment on the 15th floor of the Duarte Coelho building where "A Torre do Frevo" (The Tower of Frevo) was. She told Katarina that during a spiritual session at their house the spirit of a "master" came down to forewarn that Dona Assunção did not need to make the group parade on the streets and that she could sell all the drums from the Nação, with the exception of me—the Calunga Dona Joventina—and that I would have to be given as a gift to Katarina.

Everybody already knows the rest of the story: that Katarina accepted the honor of being my guardian and along with her husband, Bob (present here), defrayed the costs of dama de paço Lenira's education at a good high school in Recife.

Katarina wanted me to be very elegant, "full of luxury" because I really deserved it. Thus, she undid the dress she had used at Baile Municipal in 1964 and made me this beautiful dress; she ordered a velvet cape with ermines, she remade my wig that was a little spoiled, she put earrings from Toledo, Spain in my pierced ears and gave me some jewelry for my arms and neck. It was Katarina that made me this crown from a hair clip that she brought from the United States. This was incredible because she is not very skilled with her hands. She ordered a little scepter from a wood maker, and on top of the scepter she put this little animal carved from ivory.

Throughout the years I stayed with Katarina, I only appeared in public three times. The first time was in 1967 in a very beautiful ceremony held at the City Council Office when Katarina received the title "Citizen of Recife." I was by her side when she delivered her acceptance speech: "O Folclore e a Bondade Brasileira" (The Folklore and the Brazilian Kindness). Her *compadre*, Seu Luiz de França, was also there, and during an emotional beat of Baque Virado played by a maracatu group present in the room, Katarina passed me to Lenira, the young dama do paço, for her to dance with me for the last time.

The second appearance happened in 1968 at the release of the first edition of Katarina's book: *O Folclore no Carnaval do Recife* (*The Folklore in Recife's Carnival*) at Teatro Popular do Nordeste created by Hermilo Borba Filho, a person whose presence we deeply miss.

My third appearance in public was at the exhibition of Katarina Real's collection of northeastern popular art in a prominent museum in San Diego, California where I was placed right at the entrance of the exhibition with open arms welcoming the visitors from various countries of the world.

In 1968, the situation of the maracatu nations was terrible! When the great queen of Maracatu Elefante, Dona Santa, died in 1962, this group came to end; the old Estrela Brilhante became extinct in 1964; and some other maracatu groups, in precarious conditions, ran the risk of becoming extinct.

Deeply worried about this situation, Katarina, her friends João Santiago, who we deeply miss, and the president of Troça Rei dos Ciganos, the magnificent Eudes Chagas, who we also deeply miss, founded a new maracatu nação: O Porto Rico do Oriente. They were under the guidance and very generous collaboration of Katarina's *compadre*, the great master Seu Luiz de França and his exquisite batuqueiro, my friend, "Seu Veludinho" that at the time was 103 years old.

But things went very wrong in 1968! Both maracatu nação and maracatu rural groups were declining; The Federação Carnavalesca Pernambucana (Pernambucan carnival federation) was in the hands of "cartolas" (big-wigs) that barely paid attention to the problems of the carnival goers. There was an alarming lack of interest in the Pernambucan folklore and in the preservation of our regional traditions. The political situation was even worse with the dismantlement of the Movimento de Cultura Popular (Movement of Popular Culture) and so many friends were arrested, fugitives or were in exile. With much sorrow, Katarina and I left Brazil in the end of 1968, and I went to that country called the United States where nobody knows what a maracatu is, or a frevo fanfare or a dry snap from a caboclinho's *preaca*.

Katarina and I decided that I would stay there waiting for the situation for the popular traditions and for the carnival goers to get better.

In 1989, twenty years later, Katarina came back to Recife because of an invitation from Doctor Fernando Freyre, from Joaquim Nabuco Foundation to study our carnival again. She was surprised and enthusiastic by the explosive growth of popular groups of all kinds: clubes, troças, blocos, maracatus, cabloquinhos, ursos, bois and many more.

But it was just last year, in the carnival of 1995, that Katarina was so excited about the revival, restoration and renewal of so many Pernambucan folkloric traditions that she went back to Santa Fe, New Mexico, where we live and told me the following:

"Dona Joventina, I think that it is time for you to go back to your Pernambucan people to honor and thank the ones that are participating in carnival with the dozens of maracatu nations, old and new; with the hundreds of maracatu rurais, and also to honor and thank the people 'playing' with more than 300 giant puppets made by Master Sílvio Botelho and others. Also, you should thank the people who are starting new carnival clubs and singing nostalgic marches with orchestras of 'pau e corda' through the streets of the city. Thank the youth that are taking dance classes to learn frevo, maracatu, caboclinhos and all the orchestras that make a point of playing frevo on the streets during carnival instead of playing the rhythms of other countries."

On this account, folks, I am here finally with my carnival people, after almost thirty years away from this region of such invaluable folkloric cultural richness! And here, I will always be a symbol of cultural resistance and strength against everything that can harm the integrity of our carnival traditions.

To conclude, Katarina didn't want me to tell you, but it is with great sorrow that she separates from me. But she knows that I will be very well taken care of in this wonderful Museu do Homem do Nordeste (Museum of the northeastern men) of Fundação Joaquim Nabuco. I will have the calungas, dona Emília, dona Leopoldina and dom Luiz from our friend Katarina, dona Santa to make me company. Katarina promised me to come back from the United States once in a while to visit me during Momo's festivities—and I will be always waiting with much happiness the visits of all the northeastern carnival revelers here at the museum.

Thank you very much for you attention.

Katarina Real and Dona Joventina

Recife, March 5th, 1996

The Living and Changing Traditions of Maracatu de Baque Virado

Queen Marivalda, in her finery, from Maracatu Nação Estrela Brilhante. Recife 2008.

"Nagô, Nagô, nossa rainha já se coroou."
—Traditional Maracatu song

For years, most Americans have associated Brazil with samba, overlooking the numerous regional rhythms and music styles that are tremendously popular throughout Brazil. A perfect example is maracatu—a dynamic rhythm from the Northeast, propulsive and dramatic, steeped in African and Indigenous traditions, with heavy religious overtones. In the last ten years, the biggest musical success story out of Brazil has been the explosion of music from the economically impoverished, culturally rich northeast. World-famous musicians like Chico Science and the Mangue Beat movement (see "Contemporary Maracatu Manifestations" later in the book) that sprung up around him used maracatu as a springboard for contemporary fusions in the same way that Jorge Ben Jor and other MPB artists used samba a generation earlier.

Maracatu Nação or Maracatu de Baque Virado is a cultural performance that has the institution of the Kings of Congo as its "myth of origin." The institution of the Kings of Congo (or Reis Negros, i.e., Black Kings) existed in colonial Brazil from the second half of the 17th century until the abolition of slavery, in 1888. The King of Congo was a black African (slave or freeman) who acted as an intermediary between the government and the African slaves. He was expected to control and keep peace among his "pupils." From this institution, which existed throughout Brazil, different folk manifestations evolved in several regions of the country. It was in Pernambuco that the culture and music of Maracatu de Baque Virado evolved, and to this day still plays an important role in the community.

Although Maracatu de Baque Virado is a secular form of music, it has deep religious overtones. With an increasing persecution of the Catholic Church against the black community in Brazil, in the beginning of the 19th century the relationship between the black communities and the Afro-Brazilian religion became stronger and more explicit. The Maracatu Nação groups in Recife are linked to the Afro-Brazilian religion of Candomblé and the Indigenous religion of Jurema. Members of the traditional maracatu groups make regular offerings to their Orixás and often attend religious ceremonies in their *terreiros* (religious houses). Each maracatu group is connected to an Orixá and also pays tribute to their ancestors (eguns). It is important to acknowledge that participating in the religion is optional and not a requirement to take part in the percussion section of a traditional maracatu nation.

Two main entities complete a Maracatu Nação group: the court and the percussion ensemble. The court is made up of figures of the Portuguese royal court from the Baroque period and also includes dancers and figures from pre-colonial African and Indigenous traditions. The size of these maracatu courts vary among every maracatu group but can have between 20–150 or more participants. The percussion ensemble is made up of bombos (bass drums), caixas, and taróis (snare drums), bells, and various shakers. The percussion group is led by a mestre who is in charge of the musical repertoire and arrangements for the group. In most traditional maracatu groups the mestre always sings the songs while the percussionists respond to the refrains in a call-and-response form.

Maracatu Nação groups compete in every carnival in Recife downtown. For the competition the maracatu groups are divided into groups and are judged on their costumes, choreography, adornment, group size, music, and more. Two of the oldest Maracatu groups refuse to participate in this competition: Maracatu Nação Estrela Brilhante de Igarassu and Maracatu Nação Leão Coroado. Mestre Alfonso from Leão Coroado criticizes some maracatu groups for changing the character of their costumes and sound in order to shine through the competition and, ultimately, win. The competition plays a big role in the rivalry that exists among the maracatu groups. At the same time, the competition has created a common ground to these groups. Very recently, the maracatu groups that compete in the municipal competition created the Association of Maracatus Nação of Pernambuco (AMAMPE). The association was founded on August 9, 2009 with the intention of staking their claims to the government in a more collective and, consequently, effective way. The future of the association and the hopes for a more unified community remains an undefined topic; there is just the hope that maracatu gets to a status where state funding and lack of recognition from the white elite become memories of a distant past.

Maracatu: Contradictions in a Living and Changing Tradition

By Michele Nascimento

As with any art form that it is a product of an oral tradition, Maracatu de Baque Virado and its community live in a constant tension between past and present. Like traditional stories that pass on through new voices, maracatu comes to life through the voices of its living members who deal with the dilemma of passing on a tradition and living it at the same time. When traditionalists talk about Maracatu de Baque Virado, they usually evoke centuries and centuries of unrecorded and undocumented music. It is undeniable that during recent decades, more researchers have been able to record and study Maracatu de Baque Virado. Through the analysis of this research, it is noticable that even during this more recent time, which encompasses not even half of the centuries attributed to the life of maracatu, Maracatu de Baque Virado has been serving as a stage to multiple transformations. After the Mangue Beat movement, the inclusion of Maracatu de Baque Virado into the musical market not only brought more exposure to the traditional groups but also allowed outside influences to inspire changes in the traditional maracatu groups.

This is a rough presentation of the background where the discussion about the relationship between tradition and maracatu is placed. And if one still wonders why there is a soaring feeling of resentment by some purists when we talk about "changes in tradition," the answer has much to do with the understanding that Maracatu de Baque Virado is not only a rhythm but also an intricate representation of the Afro-Brazilian identity and the marginalized poor communities where it comes from. That's why admitting changes in tradition can be considered a betrayal to ancestors and to the ideologies of their communities. It is in this intricate scenario where the dilemma of the living members of a tradition is posed.

In our interviews with the mestres from the Maracatu-nação groups, it was very evident how tradition is an ongoing and very much discussed theme among them. It is such an ambivalent mode of working that even the nontraditional is presented through a traditional perspective. For instance, Mestre Shacon and Mestre Walter explained how they changed tradition using a traditional discourse. Mestre Shacon from Maracatu Nação Porto Rico introduced the atabaques (hand drums) to the sound of Porto Rico. This addition to the instrumentation gave the group a unique sound. Nevertheless, Mestre Shacon prefers to see the inclusion of atabaques not as a contemporary change in tradition but instead as a retrieval of an African influence through the hand drums very much present in the religious houses to which the maracatu groups are associated.

In our interview with Mestre Walter, contrary to Mestre Shacon he empathically declared to privilege music over religious tradition. He is the quintessential person for innovation and creativity in the current Maracatu de Baque Virado scene and has stamped his own personality in the sound of Nação Estrela Brilhante. With a long experience playing in samba groups, Mestre Walter incorporated a lot of sophisticated snare drum rolls and orchestrated ensemble breaks into Estrela Brilhante that are more common to samba. He is also responsible for including new instruments into the maracatu sound: the agbê (shekere) and, most recently, the pantagome (2010). Although he is very honest and open about musical experiments, not even Mestre Walter can detach himself from a discourse that links his contemporary adaptations to tradition. Through a traditional discourse, Mestre Walter explains that the adoption of the agbê does not go against tradition because it is an instrument used in Candomblé rituals. According to Walter, the pantagome also has its use connected to tradition since it is an instrument used in Congadas, a folkloric manifestation derived from the Kings of Congo celebrations. Mestre Walter believes that since Maracatu de Baque Virado is also linked to the Kings of Congo crowning ceremonies, the inclusion of the pantagome is surely validated from a traditional point of view. He discovered this instrument in one of his several trips to different parts of Brazil to give workshops.

The adoption of pantagome is a clear example of this new panorama in which the maracatu groups are inserted nowadays. Mestre Walter is one of the few that incorporates the changes in his music, but other mestres are also experiencing this cosmopolitan process that maracatu is going through. If in the past these groups were marginalized and isolated in their communities, nowadays they travel Brazil and the world performing and giving workshops, and more middle-class people from Recife and also foreigners are attracted to the rhythm. Obviously the group members and leaders are more exposed to many different styles of music and culture outside of their local communities. As artists and musicians it would be natural to digest these influences and express them through their music; however, this process is counter intuitive if they follow the rules of "tradition." This poses a unique challenge for most of the traditional groups: Do they adopt these influences or reject them?

Maracatu Leão Coroado and Estrela Brilhante de Igarassu, the oldest maracatu groups in Pernambuco, have been the fiercest defenders of their tradition by not allowing outside musical or cultural influences to change the group. Both groups refuse to participate in the competition promoted by Recife's City Hall during carnival because they believe that the competition is taking away the "character" of the groups by adding new elements with the purpose of winning the competition. Maracatu groups often try to recruit as many players and dancers as possible to make a larger visual and audible impact on the judges of the carnival competition. Mestre Alfonso from Leão Coroado does not believe that the higher number of players is a great addition to the sound of the ensemble, and Estrela Brilhante de Igarassu does not compete for the same reasons. Estrela Brilhante de Igarassu maintains the practices of not allowing women to play in the percussion ensemble or men to dance in the court due to their religious tradition. Both groups have been fighting against these changes, yet they continue to travel throughout Brazil and Europe while trying to maintain a healthy balance between the traditional and cosmopolitan faces of maracatu in the current times.

It seems that all of the maracatu groups interviewed for this book are in pursuit of balancing the traditional and contemporary influences within the maracatu culture. In one of our conversations with Cambinda Estrela's mestre, Ivaldo Lima, he told us that his group is completely against not allowing women and acutely affirmed that some traditions need to be broken. In the same conversation he said that he would rather not add anything new to the sound of his group and maintain the same instrumentation from the groups in the '80s. He immediately recognized his contradiction, and in a laughing manner said, "Yes, call me a contradictory man." This contradiction seems to be present in the minds of most maracatu members, leaders, batuqueiros, dancers, intellectuals, and admirers.

Out of question and contradiction is the passion for the music, culture, and the community of each of the groups we interviewed. It seems that Maracatu-Nação groups are eager to preserve something that is intangible and impossible to grasp—something that goes beyond music and carnival celebration and invokes social work, cultural identity, communal living, and that goes beyond what the word tradition means. At the same time, they also see themselves as artists in a globalized society where the lines and boundaries of what should be and what could be are constantly blurred in music and society. The maracatu musicians have the same desire of recognition in the music industry as any other bands or performing artists. This fine line between living a tradition that is constantly changing is what generates these contradictions and makes it impossible to define exactly what "tradition" is in any living art form.

Crowning Ceremonies—Rei do Congo

Maracatu de Baque Virado, as with any oral tradition, has its historical path blurred by all the voices that have tried to retell it when facing the intricate process of recreating memory. Most researchers have established a direct connection between the Maracatu de Baque Virado parades with the African Crowning Ceremonies that occurred in colonial Brazil. In order to facilitate the administration of the enslaved Africans in Brazil, the Portuguese colonizers institutionalized the Rei do Congo (King of Congo). This colonial institution was connected to the Black Catholic brotherhoods, particularly Nossa Senhora do Rosario dos Homens Pretos (Our Lady of the Rosary) in Brazil and in Portugal. The Kings of Congo were very important to the administration of the province of Brazil. The hierarchy consisted of governors, colonels, captains, lieutenants, and many more figures of the royal court. Among the African nations, the Congo Nation was the most important and carried the most power.

In the seminal book *Maracatus do Recife*, Guerra Peixe states that the Church of Our Lady of the Rosary in Recife first recorded a crowning ceremony in 1674. Nonetheless, it is possible to find an earlier description of crowning ceremonies that dates back to 1666 (by French traveler Urbain Souchu Rennefort). During these crowning ceremonies and other Catholic festivities, black people were able to connect with their African culture through music and dance. The forbiddance of using their own African costumes determined the adoption of European traditional royal attire, which can also be interpreted as a perspicacious and disguised way of mocking their oppressors. The crowning ceremonies in Recife took place in front of the Nossa Senhora do Rosario dos Homens Pretos church and provided a great opportunity for the black community to maintain their practices through singing, playing drums, and dancing under the cloak of Catholicism. The transition from the XVII century to the XIX century presents an increasing lack of leniency by the Catholic Church. The festivities and abolition of slavery in 1888 diluted any practical reasons for tolerating these celebrations. The always-present link with the Afro-Brazilian religions became more explicit as their dance, music, and singing were restricted to the social spaces of the black communities marginalized by Church and government.

The eagerness of finding in the past the same form and shape of Maracatu de Baque Virado is an equivocal and imprecise concept not only for implying the frustrating search of origins but also for the precarious information available about maracatu in colonial time. The written descriptions of the crowning ceremonies were usually given by the point of view of the white travelers and elite, who imposed their own prejudices/ignorance into their texts. On the other hand, the oral descriptions, more susceptible of changing and imprecision, have usually appeared in researches in adumbrated forms.

Most of the Maracatu de Baque Virado groups we interviewed consider the crowning ceremony of their queen (usually the religious leader of the maracatu group's *terreiro*) one of the most important elements of status for the group. This is a consequence of the intricate and close relationship between Maracatu de Baque Virado and Candomblé. Roger Bastide, a French sociologist, created the myth that the most important person in a Maracatu Nação group was the queen. Indeed, there were maracatu groups who had their queens as authority figures. Dona Santa was the most emblematic one. Upon her death in 1962, Maracatu Nação Elefante, one of the oldest maracatu groups, stopped parading at her request and had their instruments and costumes sent to the museum (you can see this material at Museu do Homem do Nordeste in Recife). Nonetheless, in the past there have also been groups presided over by men that were either religiously or financially connected to the maracatu group such as legendary master of Leão Coroado, Mestre Luís de França, who was the religious leader of Leão Coroado, and Lourenço Molla, who "purchased" Estrela Brilhante in the 1990s. Nowadays you can still see groups that are administered by powerful women such as Estrela Brilhante, Leão da Campina, Estrela Brilhante de Igarassu, and some others.

Calunga do Recife

In Recife, the calunga, also known as boneca (doll), plays a very important role in the maracatu groups. Throughout history this topic has fascinated many researchers. Mário de Andrade and many other writers have been studying the calunga dolls trying to find a lineage between their symbolism in Recife and their symbolism in Africa. For instance, in Mário de Andrade's essay "A Calunga dos Maracatus," he considers a plethora of meanings found by other etymologists for the name "calunga" to finally assert that the Bantu origin of the word would be the most valid. The word *calunga* in the Bantu dialect would have different meanings: doll, sea, Sea-God, or solely an expression of respect. Other researchers, such as Leonardo D. Silva, explain that in Africa, "calunga" implied the concept of authority, ultimately associated with religious powers. He uses this theory as a springboard to assert that, since the first half of the 19th century, the enslaved Ambundo African chiefs in Brazil secretly used the calungas to show the source of their power. Therefore, according to Silva, the calunga represented this power and unity of the African nations in Brazil. The labyrinth of hypothesis explored by the different researches incurred some mistakes (Mário de Andrade, for example, wrongly affirmed that there were only female calungas in Brazil, ignoring Calunga D. Luís from Maracatu Nação Elefante). It seems that the eagerness of finding crystalized explanations, at times, did not consider the ongoing, fast-paced changing of history and constant renewal of the meanings for the calunga doll in Brazil.

To this day, calunga dolls are part of the maracatu groups. Accepting the fact that any attempt to generalization and definition is destined for inaccuracy, I'd try to define the calunga according to how it is mostly perceived in Recife today. The calunga of Recife is considered a fetish: an object with magical powers believed to protect or aid its owner. In this sense, the maracatu groups believe that the calungas protect them from the evil spirits during the Carnaval period in Recife. They are usually black female dolls dressed in royal clothes and, in the traditional groups, made of wood. Before the Carnival period, the calunga dolls usually receive blessings/offerings and go through a religious process inside of the Candomblé house in order to lead the maracatu groups during Carnival parades. The damas-do-paço, the ones responsible for carrying the calunga, also need to go through religious preparatory rituals. In a conversation with Dona Marivalda, queen and religious leader of Maracatu Estrela Brilhante, she told us that her damas-do-paço are not allowed to drink, smoke, or have sexual intercourse until Ash Wednesday. This seems to be a common practice among most of the traditional maracatu groups. Although it is most common to see female damas-do-paço, the historian Ivaldo Lima has showed some testimonials that imply the possibility that men also held the calungas in the past.

Joventina and Erundina—Calungas in the house of Queen Marivalda, Alto Zé do Pinho, Recife, 2004.

The traditional maracatu groups "baptize" their calungas, giving names that mostly refer to the ancestors of the group also known as eguns. However, there are some exceptions to this general rule. For example: Dona Isabel, one of the calungas of Leão Coroado, is not the group's egum (ancestor). Her name refers to Princess Isabel, the one who signed the abolition of slavery in Brazil. There is also a current debate about the calungas Joventina and Erundina from Maracatu Estrela Brilhante. They are considered by the group as representations of the orixás themselves, receiving rituals related to both orixás and eguns.

Calunga Joventina is also the protagonist of a very controversial topic involving maracatu groups: Estrela Brilhante, Estrela Brilhante de Igarassu, and the American anthropologist, Katarina Real. Upon the extinction of the group Estrela Brilhante do Recife in 1966, Queen Dona Assunção gave the calunga Joventina to the anthropologist Katarina Real. After 30 years in the U.S. with the doll, Real went back to Recife to find a very different Estrela Brilhante group (none of the people from the former group were there). Katarina also became aware of the claims made by Estrela Brilhante de Igarassu about the possible stealing of Joventina from their group in the beginning of the 20th century. Both groups feel entitled to have the calunga Joventina. In the midst of this delicate situation, Katarina Real decided to give calunga Joventina to the museum. The queen of Estrela Brilhante decided to make another doll and also name her Joventina, and this is the current doll of the group. This matter is considered an unsolved problem and complicates the already delicate relationship of maracatu groups in Recife.

There is no doubt that the existence of a calunga and its indispensable connection to religion are serious matters for the maracatu groups. It seems that the calungas are not only protectors, eguns, or spiritual entities, but also a symbol of one of the most relevant elements of legitimation and spiritual symbolism of a traditional maracatu group.

The Word Maracatu

In the 19th century, the growing animosity of the Catholic Church towards the Afro-Brazilian processions and their progressive association with the Candomblé religion, grew to be strong reasons for the marginalization of maracatu groups. Through the eyes of the white elite, the gathering of Afro-Brazilian men and women was seen as a threat to society. In many newspapers from that time, one can notice that the word "maracatu" was mostly used to describe a gathering of Afro-descendants playing drums as a menacing display of immorality and barbarism. Indeed, the police's coercive power against these gatherings had increased tremendously, which made Roberto Bejamim assert that the word "maracatu" was used as a code to signal the group that the police were coming to break up their gathering. This code was announced through the sound of the drums by a rhythm that sounded similar to the word "maracatu." Guerra-Peixe, author of the famous book *Maracatus do Recife*, also pointed out that the word "maracatu" came from the nature of the rhythm. His idea was that the word represented the sound or swing of the maracatu rhythm.

On the other hand, some believe the code was actually a word uttered to signal the arrival of the police or simply the end of the dancing/singing. In the 1930s Pai Adão, an important babalorixá in Pernambuco, told researcher Gonçalves Fernandes that the code "maracatuca" meant "Let us leave," and it was used at the end of the dancing in front of the churches.

There is also Mário de Andrade's hypothesis of an indigenous origin of the word maracatu. In his book *Danças Dramáticas Brasileiras II*, Andrade said that maracatu came from the combination of the words "maraca" (indigenous instrument), "catu" ("beautiful" in Tupi), and marã (war, confusion). This theory has been disclaimed not only because of the nonexistence of a functional role of the "maraca" instrument in maracatu, but also for being highly constructed in hypothetical terms over the analysis of data collected through field research.

Another word used to refer to the traditional maracatu groups is *nação* (nation). Mestre Veludinho, one of the oldest maracatu players, told anthropologist Katarina Real that while the white elite used the word "maracatu" as a derogatory term, the slaves used the word "nação" to refer to these groups. Then, Real points out in her studies how the term "nação" reflects the diversity of ethnic groups brought from Africa to Brazil, and the power of the resistance of these groups to maintain their cultural and religious heritage. Nowadays, all of the traditional maracatu groups are formally called "Maracatu Nação" followed by the name of the group; for instance, Maracatu Nação Estrela Brilhante, Maracatu Nação Aurora Africana, etc.

Traditional Maracatu Manifestations

It's important to acknowledge before going any further in this book that there are three different styles of maracatu that are, for the most part, unrelated; Maracatu de Baque Virado (Maracatu Nação) from Recife, Maracatu Rural (Maracatu de Baque Solto) from the interior of Pernambuco in the Zona da Mata region, and Maracatu Cearense from Fortaleza in the state of Ceará. Although they share the same name, these three styles of maracatu are quite distinct musically.

Maracatu Rural, also known as Maracatu de Baque Solto or Maracatu de Orquestra, is rooted in the interior of Pernambuco and has an intimate relationship with Afro-Indigenous religion and culture in northeastern Brazil. Maracatu Rural shares very profound similarities with Maracatu Nação groups, which make some researchers believe that Maracatu Rural is the result of a parallel evolution derived from Maracatu de Baque Virado.

Maracatu Rural groups have a court and a musical ensemble known as the "Terno," but its rhythm and orchestration are strikingly different from Maracatu de Baque Virado. Maracatu Rural groups have a horn section and a much smaller percussion ensemble. The master of the group improvises rhymes and verses on top of a high-paced syncopated beat. The rehearsals (*ensaios* or *sambadas*) grow more intense before carnival period. The groups often meet in the sugarcane fields in the Zona da Mata of Pernambuco, where they compete and try to outdo one another with their rhymes and verses.

One of the most symbolic characters in a rural group is the Caboclo de Lança, a mixed race character. The Caboclo de Lança carries a lance and a large crate of bells on his back and represents a warrior. Maracatu Rural has a striking cultural similarity to the Mardi Gras Indians based in New Orleans in that many of the participants are a mixture of Indigenous and African heritage.

Maracatu Cearense is a cultural manifestation from the state of Ceará, also in the northeast of Brazil. Some researchers refuse vehemently to establish a foundational date for the maracatu in Ceará; others believe that the foundational date for the maracatu in Ceará goes back to 1936 when Raimundo Alves Feitosa, also known as Boca Aberta, went back to Ceará from Recife. He founded Nação Az de Ouro on September 6, 1936, and the group paraded for the first time in 1937.

There are two very distinct characteristics in Maracatu Cearense: transvestitism and the use of "blackface." In the beginning of the 20th century, women were not allowed to participate in maracatu groups; therefore, transvestitism became a very distinctive characteristic of this variant of Maracatu Nação. Nowadays, there is an increasing number of groups that allow women to be part of the percussion section and/or some parts of the court. It is relevant to point out that apparently the "blackface" is not viewed by its participants as a racist expression (like the American minstrel); rather, it functions as a way of paying homage to African culture.

Contemporary Maracatu Manifestations

Along with the preeminent importance of black communities' persistence in maintaining their cultural legacy, two other decisive factors were responsible for the inclusion of maracatu in the cultural market during the 1990s. The first was the creation of the *parafolclórico* group Maracatu Nação Pernambuco, and the second was the Mangue Beat movement.

Maracatu Nação Pernambuco was founded by Bernardino José da Silva Neto and other young members of Recife's middle class on December 15, 1989. The members came primarily from a dance group called Thaynahkan and paraded for the first time in Olinda in 1991. The following year, they began performing every Sunday at Mercado Eufrásio Barbosa, an important cultural center in Olinda. According to the founders and members of the group, their mission was to disseminate the very marginalized culture of maracatu to the different sectors of Pernambuco's society. During the process of adapting the maracatu performance from the streets to the stage, Maracatu Nação Pernambuco was faced with a new challenge: how to make maracatu entertaining on stage for a large audience. The group began to include complex choreography, a horn section, and other stage and instrumental elements nonexistent in traditional Maracatu de Baque Virado groups. They were very successful and toured the festival circuit in Europe and the United States. They were also one of the first groups to record and distribute a CD of maracatu. Moreover, as the group originated, not having religious ties, it established differing dynamics from the folk tradition of maracatu. It is undeniable that they contributed to the recognition of maracatu around the world as a rhythm worthy of being presented in the music market place; however, they have also been criticized for creating a misleading representation of the traditional maracatu groups.

On a less controversial path, the Mangue Beat movement also contributed greatly to the increasing interest in folk traditions of Pernambuco. Mangue Beat/Mangue Bit was a movement that arose in the beginning of the 1990s in Recife. The fundamental figures in the creation of the "Mangue" movement were Chico Science of Nação Zumbi and Fred Zero Quatro (Fred 04) of Mundo Livre S/A. The Movement fostered the development of the "new musical scene" (*nova cena musical*) of Recife, where many different local bands flourished and some became known beyond their regional borders.

As one of the Chico's lyrics said, the Mangue Beat artists had "Pernambuco bellow their feet, but their minds in the immensity of the world." They promoted the hybridism of local rhythms such as maracatu, embolada, ciranda, and coco with worldly known rhythms (rock, punk, rap, psychedelic rock, heavy metal, soul, *ragamuffin*, etc.). The anthropophagic approach of the Mangue Beat ("eating" foreign influences to create national art) is somehow similar to the approach of the musical movements of the 1970s in Brazil, such as Tropicalism. In Bahia, Tropicalism catapulted artists such as Caetano Veloso, Gilberto Gil, Gal Costa, and Maria Bethânia. Simultaneously in Recife, Alceu Valença, Robertinho do Recife, and the group Ave Sangria also used the foreign influences in the making of their sound. Journalist José Telles, in his book *Do Frevo ao Mangue*, makes a fundamental assertion about the distinction between the Mangue Beat movement and other musical Brazilian movements that dealt with the blending of influences such as the Tropicalism. Telles asserts that while Tropicalism was a superposition of types of music, Mangue Beat created a type of music of its own—a genre.

Although the Mangue Beat movement originated from a collective elaboration, most of the attention was centered in the name of Chico Science, the leader of Nação Zumbi. Chico Science was born Francisco de Assis França, to be later baptized as "Science" by Renato L. In the mid '80s Chico was part of Legião Hip Hop (Hip Hop Legion), a breakdance group very much influenced by North American black music. Later on he started his first band, Orla Orbe, which mixed elements of American funk and soul. Black music from the U.S. was also fundamental in the concept of his next band, Loustal, named after Jacques de Loustal, a French comics artist whom Chico admired. While working as a civil servant, Chico met Bola Oito, who introduced him to a samba-reggae Bahian-style group called Lamento Negro. Chico Science was from Rio Doce and Lamento Negro was from Peixinhos, two neighborhoods of Recife built on mangroves. To promote the shows of Loustal and Lamento Negro, Chico used to say, "It will be a great mud, a great swamp," which made Fred Zero Quatro call him "Mangue Boy." Later, Fred Zero Quatro used this terminology to address the participants of the Mangue Beat movement as *mangueboys* and *manguegirls*.

However, Chico Science was not satisfied with the Afro Bahian samba-reggae sound of Lamento Negro and wanted to focus on the sound of the thunderous drums of maracatu. This is when Chico took advantage of the fruitful association of Lamento Negro with Daruê Malungo, a group that worked with regional folkloric styles from the neighborhood of Chão de Estrelas, led by Mestre Gilson (also known as Mestre Meia-Noite) and his wife, Vilma Carijós. At Daruê Malungo, Chico had the opportunity to establish an in-depth relationship with the folkloric sounds of Recife that he had grown up with but were never played on the radio stations.

Maureliano Ribeiro da Silva worked at Daruê Malungo and was one of the most important bridges between Chico's rock sound and his experiments with local music. In one interview with Maureliano Silva, who nowadays makes his living primarily as a drum maker, he gave us a nonchalant explanation on how he was fundamentally responsible for the sounds that Chico Science made famous by conceptualizing the adaptation of horn sounds from James Brown's band to the drums of maracatu. Under the cloak of modern/global, the popular and folkloric music started to be consumed by middle-class people in Pernambuco.

In the book *Maracatu Atômico*, Philip Galinsky comments on the hybridism of the Mangue Beat movement. Galinsky describes how Chico Science was responsible for making the combination perfectly common straw hats (usually worn by fishermen in Recife) with hip sunglasses, lyrics with regional expressions and modern neologisms, as well as the use of hip-hop mannerisms while executing regional folkloric dance steps. Hence, Chico promoted not only a new language in music, but also showed people from his state how it was entirely possible to be regional and modern at the same time.

The first text about the Mangue Movement, which later would be called a "Manifesto," was written by Fred Zero Quatro and distributed to the Brazilian Press in 1991. The movement declared that their symbolic images were a parabolic antenna placed in the mud and a crab remixing ÁNTHENA by Kraftwerk (a Euro-tech group) on the computer. In the *Manifesto Mangue*, titled *Caranguejos Com Cerebro* (Crabs with Brains), global and modern elements are connected to the local culture (metaphorically represented by the mangroves). The manifesto explores the geographical biodiversity of Recife—a city constructed on the fertile/diverse ecosystem of mangroves—as a symbol for culture diversity as well as a reference to the serious social economical problems of this city, which had been considered by an American institution as one of the worst places to live in the world. Fred Zero Quatro was inspired by the concepts of Josué de

Castro, who wrote about his own experience growing up in the stilt houses of Recife and compared the poor men that live near the mangroves of Recife to crabs in order to discuss underdevelopment, hunger, demographic growth, and environmental problems. Much influenced by Josué de Castro's ideas, Fred Zero Quatro intertwined musical concepts with geographical and sociological considerations; however, in Fred's opinion, technology and global influence could affect social behaviors positively and needed to be used to people's advantage. The manifesto urges the participants of the movement (mangueboys and manguegirls) to inject energy into the mud to stimulate the remaining fertility of Recife and prevent its death by connecting it to the "world network."

The groundbreaking debut album *Da Lama* ao Caos (*From Mud to Chaos*) of Nação Zumbi in 1994 put into practice the concepts of Mangue Beat in music, lyrics, and visual art. After Chico Science's premature death in a car accident in 1997, the leader of Mangue Beat has almost acquired the status of a myth who has helped to burst the Pernambucan scene at a time when the music business was dominated mostly by foreign product. He became a name for a tunnel in Recife, a swamp in Olinda, and was one of the few non-Carnivalesque musicians to be paid homage during Recife's Carnival. According to many journalists and producers, Chico Science made the presence of folkloric rhythms a natural fit in the local rock festivals in Recife. Moreover, the Mangue Beat movement put Pernambuco on the world music map. Chico Science and Nação Zumbi performed at the Summer Stage in New York's Central Park in 1995, opening a show for Gilberto Gil, toured Europe, and created followers in different continents. The existence of groups such as Bloco Vomit in Scotland and Nation Beat in the U.S. prove that Chico's legacy has reached beyond the mangroves' frontiers and became a referential genre for musicians all over the world.

Noite dos Tambores Silenciosos

Noite dos Tambores Silencionsos is an event that brings together all the Maracatu de Baque Virado groups to pay tribute to their African ancestors (Eguns) through singing, dancing and playing with an ominous religious tone. The celebration is held every Monday of Carnival in front of the church Nossa Senhora do Terço. The Afro-descendant journalist Paulo Viana, who perceived Maracatu de Baque Virado as a unique symbol of Afro-Brazilian identity, envisioned the event in the 1960s. In the beginning of that decade, Viana had been gradually creating events to celebrate Afro-Brazilian culture to counter-effect the intense process of marginalization and persecution against this culture in Brazil during dictatorship. It is quite accurate to say that the '60s were a very paradoxical time to the Afro-Brazilian culture in Recife and, consequently, to the maracatu community. Despite the imminent threat of extinction pervading the maracatu scene (Maracatu Estrela Brilhante and Elefante became extinct during this decade), celebratory events were being created to honor the contribution of the African culture in Brazil. Noite dos Tambores Silenciosos was one of these events.

The ceremony begins with the presentation of traditional Maracatu Nação groups, with their respective participants (court and percussion ensemble). The drums play a prominent role in this ceremony since they serve as a medium between the material and spiritual worlds.

At midnight the ritual reaches its climax when the lights are switched off in the neighborhood of São José. The audience and performers are silent and torches are lit and carried to the doors of the church by the leaders of the maracatu groups. The silence is broken by the sound of the drums while the maracatu groups sing songs to Xangô. Each year a different religious leader is chosen to be responsible for singing the loas (laudatory songs) in homage to the Eguns.

Although this event does not date back to the previous century, it has evolved to be perceived by most maracatu members as a very significant tradition that enables them not only to pay homage to their African heritage but also to declare the importance of African religion and culture in the present time.

A maracatu batuqueiro plays barefoot during the Noite dos Tambores Silenciosos, Recife.

The Maracatu Court

The maracatu groups participate in the Carnival competition every year, marching on Avenida Dantas Barreto, Estrela Brilhante, Recife, 2007.

All of the traditional maracatu groups adapted elements of the Portuguese nobility into their culture. (To understand the possible hypothesis on how the noble court came to be used in Maracatu de Baque Virado, refer to the section "Crowning Ceremonies.") Within a traditional maracatu nation exists an entire monarchical hierarchy. Below is the list that Guerra-Peixe provided in his book *Maracatus do Recife* that describe the court of Maracatu Nação Elefante at the height of their existence when João Vitorino was the king of this nation in the 1920s.

Rainha (Queen); REI (King)

Príncipe (Prince); PRINCESA (Princess)

Duque (duke); DUQUESA (dutchess)

Conde (count); CONDESSA (countess)

Damas do Paço (Ladies of the Palace) The ones who carry the calungas.

Damas De Honra (ladies of honor)

Embaixador/Embaixatriz (ambassador) In some maracatus, he can be the man that carries the flag. In Maracatu Estrela Brilhante the ambassador is a distinct character; he takes part of the royal court. He is dressed like the nobles of Luis XV's court.

Ministro (minister of state); **Dama de Honra do Ministro** (Minister's lady of honor)

Porta-Estandarte (standard-bearer): Carries the standard of the maracatu group.

Escravo (slave): He carries the "Umbela" (a very big parasol that protects the King and the Queen).

Corneteiro (bugle player)

Secretário (secretary)

Guarda-Coroa (crown guard)

Vassalos (vassals)

Brasabundo (bodyguard)

Mestre-Sala (master of ceremonies)

Lanceiros (lance carriers) They are a group of people who carry lances and surround that African Maracatu Nation in order to protect them.

Baianas: They wear the traditional Baiana clothes (ritual clothes of the women that belong to a Candomblé).

Caboclo de Pena (indigenous): Some nations have this character in order to guide and protect them.

Batuqueiros (musicians)

During our interviews with the maracatu groups we noticed that each group has its own way of arranging its court, but overall they have the usual characters of this royal court mentioned above (queen, king, duke, duchess, ambassador, prince, princess, etc). In our interviews, the presidents of the maracatu groups didn't mention the presence of *corneteiros* (bugle players) and *brasabundos* (bodyguards). They did mention other characters not present in this list, such as dama do buquê (lady of the flowers who carries a bouquet of artificial flowers); dama da corte (lady of the court who carried the goblet); catirinas (dancers), soldados romanos (Roman soldiers); and pajens (the ones who hold the tail of the royal robes).

The most important character of the court is the queen. She is usually a yalorixá (religious leader) and is responsible for the religious aspect of the group. The queen and king usually come accompanied by the "slave" who holds the umbela (a parasol) for them. Another very important character is the dama-do-paço (lady of the palace). She is the one that holds the calunga(s) of the maracatu group and has to go through specific rituals in order to be able to carry this doll. The number of percussionists (batuqueiros) playing in the batuque (percussion ensemble) has also increased significantly over the years. According to Guerra-Peixe there were 15 batuqueiros playing in those glorious years of Maracatu Nação Elefante. Dona Marivalda (queen and president of Estrela Brilhante) told us that 100 batuqueiros played with Maracatu Nação Estrela Brilhante in the Carnival of 2011.

The Religion and Rituals of Maracatu

Central and West Africa have a predominant role in the influence of Brazilian culture due to the large number of Africans brought to Brazil at the final phase of the slave trade (18th and first half of 19th century). The eminent cultural influence of African heritage incurred the creation of various African religions developed throughout Brazil. The lineages of Candomblé are organized into *nações* (nations) loosely connected to the African ethnic place of origin. The most prevalent Candomblé nations encompass the following groups: Ketu, Ijexá, and Nagô (Yorubá groups from southwestern Nigeria and central Benin); Gêge (Ewe-Fon groups from Benin); and the Congo-Angola (Bantu groups from Central Africa). It is crucial to emphasize the African influence in Brazil dialogued with different elements creating a unique system of various religions with their own distinctive characteristics. Various syncretic forms of religion received indigenous and Afro-Brazilian elements such as *Candomblé de Caboclo* (in Bahia), *Macumba* (in Rio de Janeiro), *Umbanda* (originally from Rio de Janeiro and spread throughout Brazil), and *Jurema* (northeast of Brazil).

The Candomblé religion itself cannot be perceived as an intact set of beliefs transplanted from Africa, as it suffered the influences from the environment of the New World. For instance, the cult of warrior gods, such as Ogum, acquired much more relevance on the Brazilian side of the Atlantic where the overbearing presence of the Catholic Church and colonial power prevailed. The association of the orixá gods with Catholic saints was a consequence of this mixed environment permeated by an intense persecution against the Afro-Brazilian community. The increasing brutality against the Afro-Brazilian religions did not prevent the growth of Candomblé houses throughout Brazil. In Recife, the Candomblé houses, which began to appear during colonial times founded by slaves and free blacks, did not diminish in number over time. They were initially predominantly located in the downtown area of the city; however, by the early 20th century, more Candomblé houses were founded by former slaves and free blacks in low-income communities in the outskirts of the city.

It is around this time, late 19th century (after abolition of slavery) and beginning of the 20th century, that the relationship between the maracatu groups and religion became more explicit. The members of the black community had to disguise their religious ritual as Carnival Maracatus in order to avoid the persecution of church and state. Along with the Afro-Brazilian religions, maracatu went through a long period of marginalization, and until today most of the groups were located in the low-income black communities in Recife. Nowadays, the association of a Maracatu Nação with a Candomblé house is indispensable to the recognition of a group with such status.

The *pai-de-santo* (father of saints), the leader of the Candomblé, defines a follower's future by rolling the buzios (shells), in Bomba de Hemeterio, Recife, 2005.

Nagô is the predominant Candomblé nation in the state of Pernambuco, and it reveals specific characteristics in its set of principles. A pungent characteristic of Candomblé is its universalism. Although it is usually connected to an African identity, everybody, independently from racial or economic backgrounds, is a "daughter" or "son" of the orixás. The orixás are connected to the forces of nature with human qualities and associated to colors, food, dance, and music. The Candomblé house is usually called *terreiro* (in Recife also known as *Xangô*, an orixá that acquired great importance in Candomblé practice in the region), and their religious leaders are called *babaloriás* (priests) and *yalorixás* (priestesses). Music and dancing are fundamental in the cult of the orixás and the process of reaching the spiritual world. Understanding the musical influences of the polyrhythmic call-and-response formatted songs of Candomblé helps a great deal to the learning of maracatu as a musical rhythm. In Recife, some of the leaders of the maracatu percussion ensembles are also the leading drummers (called *ogans*) of the maracatus' Candomblé house. In Candomblé the drumming part is restricted to males who must go through specific religious rituals to be able to play. Unlike the dancers, they do not go through the process of being possessed by the spiritual entities.

The drums are blessed and their making also involves religious rituals. There are three drums: the lowest-pitched (and largest) drum played by the leading drummer, the medium-pitched drum, and the highest-pitched drum. Completing the set of musical instruments of

Candomblé are two other instruments: the agogô (bell) and the agbê (shaker). In Recife the drums (called *Ilu*) are made of plywood material with a double-headed cylinder shape. The goatskin is placed on the head and tensioned with metal rims and bolts on the side. There are records indicating that in the past these drums were made of barrel/solid wood and tensioned with rope.

Most of the language of the music comes from an inspiration that arises in the *terreiros*. For instance, Mestre Shacon Viana told us that he was inspired by the divisions of the ilu and translated them to the secular maracatu drums, calling them: *melê*, *biancô*, *ian*, and *iandarrum*. Nowadays, percussionists and even masters of the percussion ensemble of a Maracatu Nação group don't have to belong to the religion, but it is undeniable that the syncopated groove comes from the Afro-Brazilian religion.

In Recife, the deep connection of the maracatu groups with the Candomblé religion is unquestionable. The same is not true when we deal with the status of the Jurema religion. The cult of Sacred Jurema and its role in the maracatu groups are still controversial topics in Recife. In order to understand the root of the controversy, one needs to be aware of what Jurema cult implies. The name Jurema refers to the sacred plant from whose roots the Indigenous people in the northeast of Brazil produced a hallucinogenic drink that favors the connection with a spiritual world. Through our interviews with the Maracatu Nação groups, we noticed that there was a unanimous involvement of the members of religious houses with the Jurema sect; however, they all explained their connection to it in different ways. Some groups understood Jurema as an element intertwined to their maracatu, and others perceived it as a parallel cult to their main Nagô Candomblé beliefs. It seems the affirmation of the Afro-Brazilian matrix for the Maracatu Nação groups is more relevant or accurate (depending on how one wants to perceive it) than the indigenous-based sect of Jurema in terms of legitimizing their identity.

The *terreiros* in Recife, in their intricate configurations, cannot be considered solely as religious houses; they function as social spaces that express through dance, music, and beliefs the communal ethos in which Maracatu de Baque Virado is rooted.

The ceremony of releasing the calungas (dolls), in the terreiro of the Maracatu Nação Estrela Brilhante, in Bomba do Hemeterio, Recife, 2006.

Maracatu Nação Porto Rico

Maracatu Nação Porto Rico is located in the neighborhood of Pina, in the southern part of Recife. The history and origins of the maracatu are disputed, though most members of the group state that Nação Porto Rico was founded in the city of Palmares, Pernambuco in 1916. After a brief disappearance, the group reemerged in Água Fria (a neighborhood in Recife) under the guidance of Zé da Ferida. Due to lack of social support in a time of severe political and social prejudice in the 1950s, the group was dissolved. In 1967 the group was resurrected with the name Porto Rico do Oriente under newly crowned king and mestre José Eudes Chagas, with help from Katarina Real, Luís de França, and Seu Veludinho. After the death of Eudes Chagas in 1978, the group disbanded once again until the appointment of yalorixá Elda Viana as queen in 1980.

Despite their checkered past, Porto Rico has established itself as one of the most well-known maracatu groups in the world. A significant reason for the success of the group is the musical direction of Jailson Viana Shacon, or simply Mestre Shacon. He is the son of queen Elda Viana and became the mestre in 1999, replacing Mestre Jaime. Mestre Shacon has introduced many new toadas (songs) currently used by the group, and is responsible for bringing the atabaque and timbal (instruments used in Candomblé) to the maracatu rhythm. Though there is strong criticism from tranditionalists, the sound of the atabaques gives the group a very unique groove. Mestre Shacon, who is an alabê (the most important player of Porto Rico's religious house), toured Brazil playing cavaquinho prior to becoming mestre. In our interview with him, he said he learned how to play cavaquinho (a ukulele-like instrument used in samba and pagode) by ear and prefers calling his players "musicians" instead of "batuqueiros" (the typical designation given to players in a maracatu group). Shacon is credited with producing both albums for Maracatu Porto Rico: *No Baque das Ondas* (2000) and *Noite do Dendê* (2009).

Nação Porto Rico is linked to the Candomblé religion, but the elements of Jurema Sagrada are also present. Mestre Shacon explains the presence of Jurema using a concept he calls "Paralelo singular" (unique parallel). In his opinion, the elements of Jurema are used mainly in the most profane part of maracatu, in other words, when the groups are parading on the streets. Porto Rico's religious house belongs to the denomination of gegê-nagô (tribes from Africa). There are three calungas in Nação Porto Rico: Dona Inês, Dona Elizabete, and Dona Bela; the last one is a witch cloth doll ("bruxa de pano").

Religion is also very relevant in Mestre Shacon's creative process for composing his songs. According to Mestre Shacon, the first toada he composed as the mestre of Porto Rico was a gift from the orixás and plots a conversation between two orixás: Xangô and Omulu.

Maracatu Nação Estrela Brilhante do Recife

Nação Estrela Brilhante is considered one of the most accomplished maracatu groups, both within Recife and worldwide. Since 2000, Estrela Brilhante has traveled to Europe and other parts of Brazil to present workshops on their dance and percussion styles. Estrela's past is as turmultuous as any other maracatu group, reemerging from numerous disappearances since their founding in 1906. The group was founded in the neighborhood of Campo Grande by Mestre Cosme Damião Tavares, known as Seu Cosmo, a fisherman from Igarassu who migrated to Recife. After his death in 1955, his widow, Dona Assunção, became responsible for the group until 1966, when the group stopped parading due to financial problems. Around 1973, Maria Madalena, yalorixá and former queen of Maracatu Leão Coroado, along with José Martins de Albuquerque, helped Estrela Brilhante obtain a respectful status in Recife's Carnival scene. At this time, Maracatu Estrela Brilhante was located in the community of Alto do Pascoal-Água Fria in northern Recife.

In the early '90s, Martins de Albuquerque, the President of Estrela Brilhante, had health problems and the group started to decline. Then Lourenço Molla bought Estrela Brilhante's belongings from Martins de Albuquerque and moved the group to the community of Padre Lemos in the neighborhood of Casa Amarela. Lourenço Molla, along with dissidents from Leão Coroado, Gigante do Samba group, and other members of Casa Amarela's community, helped in the beginning of a successful path for the current Estrela Brilhante group. Molla left the group in 1995 and Marivalda Maria dos Santos, queen and religious leader of the maracatu during Molla's time, became president of the group. The headquarters of the Nação Estrela Brilhante relocated to Marivalda's house in Alto José do Pinho (another community in the neighborhood of Casa Amarela), and she was officially crowned queen in 2002. Walter de França, mestre of Nação Estrela Brilhante, joined the group during Molla's presidency, and just like Dona Marivalda he had come from Maracatu Nação Leão Coroado. Mestre Walter is one of the most innovative mestres of traditional maracatu to this day. Besides introducing new instruments to the maracatu rhythm, he is also responsible for introducing many complex breaks for his drummers to play (as can be found in samba schools, where Walter was brought up).

Maracatu Nação Aurora Africana

The only maracatu on record in the city of Jaboatão dos Guararapes, Maracatu Nação Aurora Africana, was founded on August 8, 2001. They began performing in 2003, and in 2004 they first participated in, and won, the Recife Carnival competition for category B. In 2005 there was a flood in Jaboatão dos Guararapes that destroyed many houses and also 70 percent of the group's costumes. Since then, they have been more focused on doing community-oriented projects. Fábio Sotero is one of the founders, the current president, and also the standard-bearer of the group. In our interview he emphasized the importance of the community outreach programs of the group. Maracatu Nação Aurora Africana has its headquarters in the neighborhood of Vila Rica close to the religious house of their queen, Gilvanice Conceição de Lima, also known as Mãe Gilva. Her religious house is gegê-nagô, and she is responsible for the religious aspect of the group. Mãe Gilva has been the queen of the group since its foundation.

Currently Aurora Africana has only one calunga, Dona Cleonice, though Fábio notes they are waiting on the "approval" of the orixás in order to have another calunga. According to Fábio, the major orixás of the nation are Iansã and Ogum; however, the religious aspect of Aurora Africana is a mixture of many religions. They not only praise the orixás of Candomblé but are also connected to the rituals of Jurema and Umbanda. The Jurema entity that protects the group is Cabocla Aurora, and the colors of the group are red and white. As found in many other groups, not all the members need to be connected with the religion, though important court characters such as the queen, king, damas do paço, and the mestre of percussion must be involved in the religious rituals.

The relationship between the music and the instruments is strongly emphasized in Aurora Africana. The tambores of the group are made of macaíba (Fábio assures that they do not cut the trees down), and the bombos mestres (the biggest drums) go through a religious ritual and can only be played by chosen players. The rest of the instruments do not necessarily go through a religious ceremony, and all the instruments are made by the members of the group except for the caixa and tarol. The percussionists are led by mestre Alessandro Barros, son of Mãe Gilva.

Maracatu Nação Raízes de Pai Adão

The terreiro (Candomblé house) of Pai Adão is one of the most reknowned religious temples in Brazil. It was founded by Inês Joaquina da Costa, also know as Ifa Tinuké, in the second half of the 19th century. The terreiro rose to fame with Felipe Sabino da Costa, better known as babalorixá Pai Adão, in the beginning of the 20th century. After his death in 1936, his son José Romão Felipe da Costa, followed by Malaquias Felipe da Costa, became responsible for the house. Today the children of Malaquias run the terreiro of Pai Adão, which is located in Água Fria, Recife.

The maracatu group was founded on January 20, 1998 by Inaldo Costa Nascimento, Tomé Gomes da Costa, Itaiguara Felipe da Costa, and Maria do Bonfim. According to Itaiguara, who is the current president of the group, they formed the maracatu to pay homage to Pai Adão and all of his contributions to the African culture in Brazil. The group is deeply connected to both the Candomblé religion and to the Jurema. Itaiguara explained that the Jurema cult was influenced by indigenous ancestors that became part of the family.

The group has two calungas, Alexandrina and Vicentina, which pay homage to two very important women of the family. Alexandrina Felipe da Costa was Pai Adão's wife as well as the oldest religious daughter of Inês. Maria Vicentina da Costa was the wife of Pai Adão's son, Malaquias, and also the adopted daughter of Inês. Calunga Alexandrina represents orixá Oxum. Calunga Vicentina represents orixá Iemanjá, who is also the orixá patroness of the Candomblé house and the maracatu group.

The court is led by queen Nina and king Roberto, and the percussion group is led by Mestre Leandro. In our interview with the president and master of the group, both declared that the emergence of Mangue Beat was very influential to their involvement with maracatu. Raízes de Pai Adão is a perfect example of how much the tradition, represented by their religious legacy, and the new influences in the music community intricately co-exist in the culture of Recife.

Maracatu Nação Cambinda Estrela

According to Mestre Ivaldo Marciano de França e Lima, the journey of Cambinda Estrela is very controversial. Records show that Cambinda Estrela converted from playing Maracatu Rural to Maracatu de Baque Virado (and thus became a nação) around 1947, although the date given by its first president, Manoel Martins, was 1953. Mestre Ivaldo believes that the controversy about the "origins" of Nação Cambinda Estrela is connected to the lack of clear divisions between these two types of maracatu in the past. That's why Mestre Ivaldo prefers to talk about the history of his group from October 2, 1997, when he and Pai Gerivaldo decided to start a new maracatu group.

In this year Mestre Ivaldo and Pai Gerivaldo were awarded Cambinda Estrela group ("inactive" since the beginning of the 1980s) by the Federação Carnavalesca (Recife Carnival's Association). In 1998 the group started participating in Recife's Carnival to later win the category B competitions in the years 1999 and 2000. Maracatu Nação Cambinda Estrela is unique in that its headquarters is located in the community of Chão de Estrelas, in northern Recife; however, the group is also affiliated with the communities of Capilé, Bom Clima, Areeiro, and Sotave.

The principle ideals of the group are fighting against racism and homophobia as well as fighting for education for the poor and more social equality. The administrative structure of the group also follows a very intricate system in order to accommodate so many different community leaders. Instead of having one director/president, there are three main administrative branches: a board of directors, an advisory board (that can block any decision made by the board of directors), and a general assembly consisting of the members of the group. The two calungas of Cambinda Estrela, Dona Aurora and Dona Inês, remain in Chão de Estrelas, which is a matter of dispute among the communities that argue that the calunga should go to all the religious houses of the different communities. Mestre Ivaldo emphasizes that the social and political work is more of a priority than the religious commitments and the musical aspect of the group.

Cambinda Estrela is unique in that they parade with a great number of mineiros (see instrument list for description). Lima attributes this peculiarity in the instrumentation of the group to a mere financial decision, since mineiros are the most inexpensive instruments, and the group is committed to lending the instruments free of charge for people to play in the parades. In our interview, Mestre Ivaldo asserted: "We do not choose rhythmic quality over social inclusion." Though musicality is not the top priority, the uniqueness of their sound and arrangements make Cambinda Estrela a necessary study when examining maracatu in Recife.

Maracatu Nação Estrela Brilhante de Igarassu

One of the oldest folkloric groups in Brazil, Maracatu Estrela Brilhante de Igarassu is considered the oldest Maracatu de Baque Virado group. Henry Koster, a German researcher, was one of the first to write about the existence of this maracatu group at a crowning ceremony on the Island of Itamaracá in the beginning of the 19th century. The members of the group claim that Estrela Brilhante de Igarassu was founded on December 8, 1824, on the island of Itamaracá by João Francisco da Silva. Seu Neusa, son of João Francisco, and his wife Mariú later moved the group to Alto do Rosário in the city of Igarassu. After Seu Neusa's death in the 1980s, the group stopped parading. Later in 1994, Dona Olga, one of Seu Neusa's daughters, brought back Estrela Brilhante de Igarassu to the streets of Pernambuco. Dona Olga is the current queen and president of the group, and her youngest son, Gilmar de Santana, is the mestre. Dona Olga says that maracatu is a family matter for them and she wants to keep its traditions intact. According to Dona Olga, women cannot play and men cannot dance due to religious traditions.

The group is connected to the Candomblé religion of the Nagô sect having the Orixá Xangô as its protector. Although Dona Olga pays her "dues" to the Jurema religion, the members insist that the connection to Jurema does not pertain to the maracatu group but only to Dona Olga personally. According to Dona Olga's son, Gilberto José de Santana, most of the current members of the group are not connected to the Candomblé religion, and only the core members are responsible for the religious part of the maracatu group. These core members also believe that the religious traditions are important to the sound of the group, and that's why they make their drums go through religious rituals. The group currently has one calunga, Dona Emilia, referred by Dona Olga as "the owner of the group."

In 2009, Estrela Brilhante de Igarassu received the title of "Living Cultural Patrimony" from the state of Pernambuco for its contribution to popular culture in the state.

Maracatu Nação Leão Coroado

According to Leão Coroado's bylaw, this group was founded on December 8, 1863 by Manoel Benedito da Silva, Laureano Manoel dos Santos, and Manoel Machado de Souza. The group was founded in the neighborhood of Boa Vista in Recife, on Leão Coroado Street, from where it took its name. Maracatu Nação Leão Coroado is considered the oldest maracatu nation that has been playing without any interruptions in its history (other maracatu groups were forced to stop playing for some years due to financial problems). Although Leão Coroado was founded in Boa Vista, it has had its headquarters in many different neighborhoods: São José, Afogados, and Vila São Miguel. The most famous queen of Maracatu Leão Coroado was the legendary Maria Júlia do Nascimento, also known as Dona Santa.

Maracatu Nação Leão Coroado also gave lengendary musicians to the maracatu community. One of the most famous maracatu percussionists was João Batista de Jesus, also known as Seu Veludinho, who died in 1996 when he was 110 years old. His wisdom and knowledge of Maracatu de Baque Virado has been recognized by the whole maracatu community in songs and literature related to the topic. Mestre Luiz de França was another very important person for Maracatu Leão Coroado. He was born in 1901 and died in 1997 after being the administrative, religious, and musical leader of his group for 43 years. Mestre Luís de França was an oluô (the highest religious position in the nagô sect), and his Pais de Santo (spiritual leaders) were Eustachio Gomes de Almeida and Dona Santa. Mestre Luís de França never wanted to be the king of Leão Coroado, making history as one of the few mestres that were respected religious and musical leaders of a traditional maracatu group. As a recognition to Mestre Luís' contribution to Pernambuco's culture, the state government chose his birthday, August 1, to celebrate the "Day of Maracatu" in the state. Mestre Luís de França chose the young babalorixá of the nagô sect, Afonso Aguiar, to be his successor. After Luís de França's death, Mestre Afonso took over the religious and musical responsibilities of Maracatu Nação Leão Coroado, and the headquarters of Leão Coroado was transfered to Mestre Afonso's Candomblé house in Águas Compridas, Olinda.

Maracatu Leão Coroado has two calungas: Dona Clara and Dona Isabel. Dona Clara represents an ancestor of the group, but Dona Isabel represents the princess who signed the abolition of slavery papers in Brazil. There's an emblematic story about the importance of the calungas for a traditional maracatu group involving Dona Clara and Dona Isabel. In the 1970s during a flood that destroyed a lot of houses in Recife, mestre Luís de França left all of his belongings at his house but made sure he rescued the two calungas of Leão Coroado.

In 2005, the State of Pernambuco granted Leão Coroado the title of "Living Cultural Patrimony" for its contributions to the preservation of Maracatu de Baque Virado.

Maracatu Nação Leão da Campina

On the wave of the new groups that took advantage of a more propitious scenario, Maracatu Nação Leão da Campina hit Recife's shore in the '90s. On a very symbolic tone, the emblematic year of the death of Chico Science was also the year of the birth of a new maracatu nation. Located initially in the neighborhood of Coelhos in Recife, Maracatu Nação Leão da Campina was founded by Aécio da Hora on July 26, 1997 and had strong connections with a dance company at that time. Nowadays the group is located in Ibura (another neighborhood in Recife) and has come a long way since 1997. As a matter of fact, if one takes under consideration the competition promoted by Recife's City Hall, Maracatu Nação Leão da Campina's path to success is undeniable. On the sixth birthday of their existence they jumped to category A of this competition, and in 2007 they came in second place in this category. Leão da Campina is under the guidance of Nadja Cristina de Castro, also known as Mãe Nadja. She has been the queen, president, and religious leader of the group since 1998. Mãe Nadja has a religious house called Abassá Axé Oya Balé Omim from the Angola Nation. The Angola nation is not very common in Pernambuco, as she stated in our interview. In this religion she is the "daughter" of Mércia da Oxum Akarê, matriarch of the Angola nation in Pernambuco, who died in 2010 leaving Mãe Nadja as the heiress of her religious house. The group has three calungas: Maria Luisa; Ana Rosa, and Rita de Cássia that we met at the Candomblé house located not very far from the headquarters of the group. The Ogans, in the Angola Nation, are called tata ngomas (Ogans are the people responsible for playing drums in a candomblé house).

Mãe Nadja was crowned on May 21, 2004 and has been guiding her group to what she considered a very successful path. In our interview she took pride on the various groups under her sponsorship and the different social outreach activities promoted in the community by Maracatu Nação Leão da Campina. Mãe Nadja considers herself an innovator. She introduced new characters to her maracatu group such as: odaliscas, soldados romanos, aias, aio, and bandus. Her son Hugo Leonardo is the current mestre of Maracatu Leão da Campina.

THE MUSIC of MARACATU DE BAQUE VIRADO

Mestre Walter at rest at the school he teaches. Bomba de Hemeterio, Recife, 2005.

"I don't care about how tradition tells you to play,
I just want it to sound and feel good!"
—Mestre Walter

CHAPTER 1

Mineiro, Agbê, and Gonguê

Let's get started with the high-pitched instruments of a traditional maracatu group. It's important to point out that you won't hear all of these instruments in every traditional maracatu group. Each group has its own preference and historical reasons why they choose to play or not play some of these instruments. Take the agbê, for instance. This instrument is commonly heard in Nação Estrela Brilhante do Recife and Nação Porto Rico, while many of the other traditional maracatu groups never play it. Mestre Walter brought the agbê into Estrela Brilhante for the first time in the early 1990s and claimed it was a traditional maracatu instrument because of its use in Candomblé ceremonies. Prior to this, the agbê was not considered a traditional maracatu instrument. Since then, however, many of the traditional maracatu groups have adopted the instrument into their sound.

Below are examples of the basic patterns and grooves played on these instruments. It's important to start with these instruments and develop a strong groove on them before moving on to the other instruments, since these provide the basic foundation of the maracatu rhythm.

All examples are recorded at 95 bpm.

Mineiro Example 1: Here is a basic pattern for the mineiro. Pay close attention to the accents, and practice playing this groove with both a straight feel and a lilt. This is a universal mineiro pattern that you'll hear played by many of the traditional nations such as Estrela Brilhante, Leão Coroado, and Porto Rico.

TRACK 1
0:00–0:13

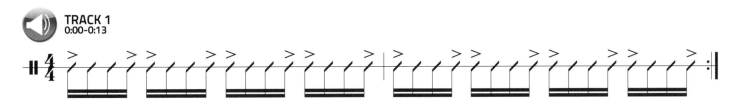

Mineiro Example 2: This is a mineiro variation that you'll also hear most of the traditional nations play.

TRACK 1
0:14–0:26

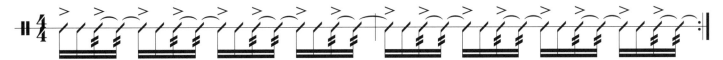

Mineiro Example 3: Cambinda Estrela. Here you'll notice that Cambinda Estrela plays the mineiro with the exact same rhythm that the agbê is played by other groups.

TRACK 1
0:27-0:41

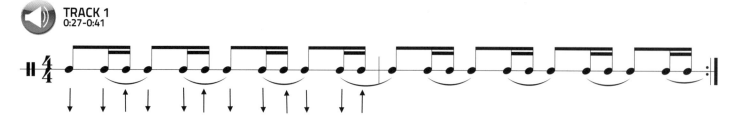

Example 4: Agbê: In this example, the pattern starts with an upward motion, though some maracatu groups start with a downward motion. Practice playing both ways.

TRACK 2

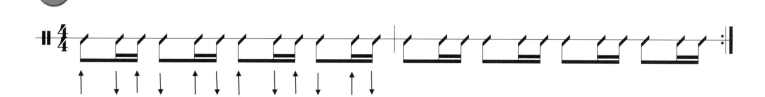

Basic Gonguê Bell Pattern: This is the clavé of maracatu. Learn this rhythm and internalize it before going any further into this book. This gonguê pattern is the point of gravity for every maracatu rhythm in this book. Practice playing the gonguê while singing the other maracatu patterns from this book at the same time.

TRACK 3

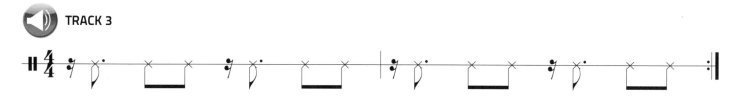

Gonguê Variations. It's important to point out that gonguê players never stick to just one pattern. They constantly improvise around the basic pattern, helping create more energy and forward motion in the music. Here are a few basic variations to check out. Once you feel comfortable with all of them, try going in and out of each variation without stopping. This will help you play the gonguê freely and will also help you develop your own vocabulary on the instrument. Just make sure when you start improvising, your variations always relate to the basic gonguê pattern (clavé) above. Everything must revolve around this basic gonguê rhythmic cell in order for the groove to be happening.

Gonguê Variation 1

TRACK 4
0:00-0:12

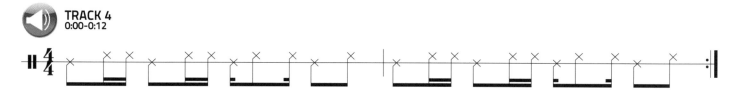

Gonguê Variation 2

 TRACK 4
0:13-0:25

Gonguê Variation 3

 TRACK 4
0:26-0:38

Gonguê Variation 4: The following two examples were played by Nação Cambinda Estrela during the interviews for the research for this book.

 TRACK 4
0:38-0:51

Gonguê Variation 5: Nação Cambinda Estrela

 TRACK 4
0:51-1:05

Gonguê Variation 6

Gonguê Variation 7

Gonguê Variation 8

Playing the gonguê during the Carnival competition on Avenida Dantas Barreto, Recife, 2007.

CHAPTER 2

Baque de Luanda/Baque de Marcação

This chapter will cover the most common maracatu groove, Baque de Marcação, which translates literally to "Marking Beat." You will hear almost every traditional maracatu group from Recife play this groove or some variation of it. Most groups actually call this groove Baque de Luanda (Beat of Luanda), referring to the capital of Angola. It's essential that you have a strong understanding of marcação or luanda before moving on to any of the following chapters, since most of the other maracatu grooves are variations on this one.

Despite the disagreement over the name of this rhythm, the actual groove is the same, and these examples will provide you with a foundation and the vocabulary necessary for understanding and playing with any traditional maracatu group from Recife. Here's a list of a few of the traditional maracatu nations who play this groove:

- Maracatu Nação Estrela Brilhante
- Maracatu Nação Leão da Campina
- Maracatu Nação Porto Rico
- Maracatu Nação Aurora Africana
- Maracatu Nação Raízes de Pai Adão

Caixa Pattern for Baque de Marcação: RRLR-RLRL

The caixa examples below are some of the basic patterns for playing Baque de Marcação with Nação Estrela Brilhante. You'll notice a striking similarity in this sticking pattern with a lot of the New Orleans second-line snare patterns that Stanton Moore talks about in his book *Take It to the Street*. We will explore some of these similarities in more depth later in this book in the drumset sections, but for now let's start off by working on the sticking patterns, feel, accents, and the roll variations for the caixa.

Try practicing these caixa grooves with varying degrees of swing, from a straight feel all the way to a hard swing feel, similar to samba. Some traditional maracatu groups play their caixa patterns with more lilt than others. You'll want to be able to play all of the caixa parts between each extreme of straight and swung in order to develop an understanding of each maracatu group and their swing feel. Make sure to practice these examples with a metronome. Start off very slow, take your time, and focus on your feel.

Caixa Variation 1: This is a very basic foundation for starting to learn the maracatu caixa groove. Once you're comfortable with this one, move on to the following caixa grooves with rolls.

All caixa examples 107 bpm.

TRACK 5
0:00–0:11

Caixa Variation 2

TRACK 5
0:12-0:23

R R L R R L R L L R R L R R L R   R R L R R L R L R R L R R L R

Caixa Variation 3

TRACK 5
0:24-0:36

R R L R R L R L R R L R R L R L   R R L R R L R L R R L R R L R L

Nação Estrela Brilhante—Baque de Marcação

Mestre Walter leads Maracatu Nação Estrela Brilhante during the Carnival competition on Avenida Dantas Barreto, Recife, 2007.

"You can't use that drumset technique when playing the maracatu caixa. It's too clean and doesn't sound right!"—Mestre Walter

That's what Mestre Walter told me while I was hanging out at his house studying some of the caixa parts with him. I was holding the sticks with a traditional grip, which obviously wasn't getting the sound he wanted. There's really something to be learned from this statement, and the same thing applies to all genres or styles of music. The technique (or lack thereof) has a lot to do with the sound that you will pull out of your instrument. Certain styles of music require a very clean, articulated sound, while others rely on the dirt and grit generated by loose articulation. The latter happens to be the case for maracatu. Don't make your rolls super clean. They should buzz and crush and sound like they just came out of the swamps. Check out the transcription of Mestre Walter's caixa example below, and make sure your rolls are as dirty as you can make them.

Mestre Walter: Caixa Pattern for Baque de Marcação

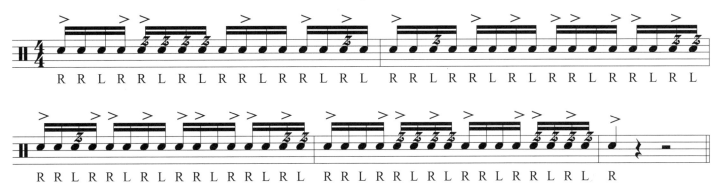

Caixa Variation 4

TRACK 6
0:00–0:11

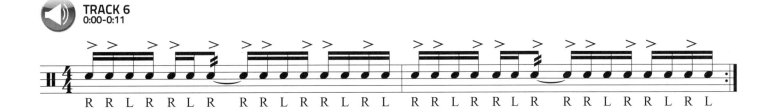

Caixa Variation 5

TRACK 6
0:12–0:23

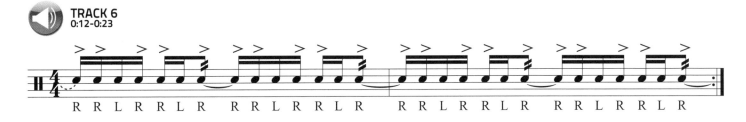

Caixa Variation 6

TRACK 6
0:24–0:36

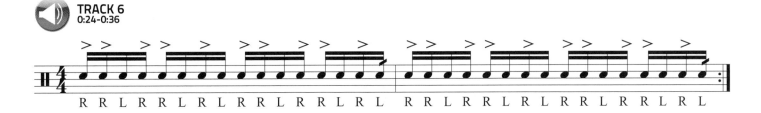

Baque de Marcação: Alfaia

Here is the basic alfaia pattern for Baque de Marcação. It's very important to pay close attention to the accents in this groove. With the exception of some maracatu groups, like Nação Leão Coroado who use a large mallet in both hands, the "strong" hand always holds a large wooden mallet while a smaller stick is often held in the "weak" hand, therefore further emphasizing the accents in this groove. The "weak" hand notes should be practiced as if they were ghost notes, being felt more than heard.

 **TRACK 7**

Here is a score view of how the caixa and alfaia parts look together. In a traditional maracatu setting there are three ways of starting a groove:

1. With a song (toada or loa). The song has a melodic cadence that calls the drummers in to begin the groove

2. The caixa plays a chamada (roll-off or call) that calls the drummers into the groove in the instance of playing an instrumental arrangement

3. Sometimes you'll hear a group use a combination of the song and the caixa chamada to call the drummers in as well.

Nação Cambinda Estrela and Nação Encanto da Alegria are examples of traditional maracatu groups that use this combination of melody and caixa chamada to call the drummers in.

The example below is a basic chamada for Baque de Marcação. There is not really a strict tempo at the beginning of the chamada and there is never a count-off. The chamada often starts off with a very relaxed feeling, and the tempo gradually builds faster starting around measure three and often has a strong acceleration on measure five. This is done through intuition by the musicians, and each traditional maracatu group has its own unique way of accelerating during the chamada.

There is no metronome count-off in the following chamada example; however, I've given you two stick clicks on the audio track so you can prepare to play along.

Baque de Marcação with caixa chamada as played by Nação Estrela Brilhante

🔊 TRACK 8

🔊 TRACK 9

Track 9 is "Estrela Brilhante é Um Brilho" by Nação Estrela Brilhante from the Nation Beat CD *Maracatuniversal*. I stripped all of the instruments so you can hear just Mestre Walter and Estrela playing Baque de Marcação.

* Lyrics to this song can be found at www.maracatuny.com

Nação Porto Rico—Baque de Luanda

Now let's take a look at how Nação Porto Rico plays this same rhythm. First, they call this rhythm Baque de Luanda, not Baque de Marcação. Luanda is the capital of Angola and is believed to be one of the main places from where slaves were brought to the state of Pernambuco.

It's also important to point out that Nação Porto Rico uses a caixa and a tarol. These two instruments are very similar; however, the tarol is generally tuned higher than the caixa, which is deeper and tuned more like a regular snare drum. Notice that these caixa and tarol parts are all played hand-to-hand, and there aren't any crush rolls like in Estrela Brilhante's style of playing the caixa.

All Porto Rico examples are at 98 bpm.

Nação Porto Rico Caixa Example 1

TRACK 10
0:00–0:10

Nação Porto Rico Caixa Example 2

TRACK 10
0:11–0:22

Once you have a strong understanding of the caixa and tarol parts, try putting them together along with the alfaia groove. As I said in the "Performance Notes" section of this book it's best to practice this material with friends. You'll need at least two other people to play these three parts to hear how they sound together. Or you can try using a loop station or any type of recording program to create loops of each section, enabling you to play different parts on top of each other. This is a good way to practice getting your technique down, but I suggest playing with other people as often as possible.

A very important note about the alfaia for Nação Porto Rico: The left hand (the weak hand) is always played holding a small twig rather than a stick. This stick is called the *rebate* (pronounced hay-ba-tee). Porto Rico does not emphasize the left hand as much as some of the other maracatu groups, like Estrela Brilhante. This creates even more emphasis on the accented parts of the groove.

Members of Maracatu Nação Porto Rico play at the abertura (opening) of Carnival at Marco Zero, Recife, 2005.

Baque de Luanda as played by Nação Porto Rico: Caixa, Tarol, and Alfaia

 TRACK 11

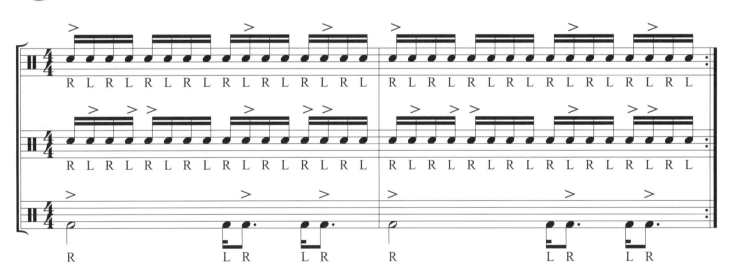

Nação Porto Rico Entrada for Baque de Luanda with Caixa, Tarol, and Alfaia

Now let's put all of these parts together. The tarol, caixa, and alfaia parts all have an entrance. Previously in this chapter we took a brief look at the Estrela Brilhante "chamada," or call, which brings in all of the instruments. Nação Porto Rico plays a similar entrance; however, they call this the "Entrada." This can get confusing because Porto Rico also has a chamada that is completely different, and we'll look at that in a minute. But first let's take a look at the entrada using the caixa and tarol. Pay very close attention to the melodic interaction happening between the caixa, tarol, and alfaia parts.

There is no metronome count-off in the following chamada example because there is an acceleration in tempo during the chamada. I've given you two stick clicks so you can prepare to play along with this track.

TRACK 12

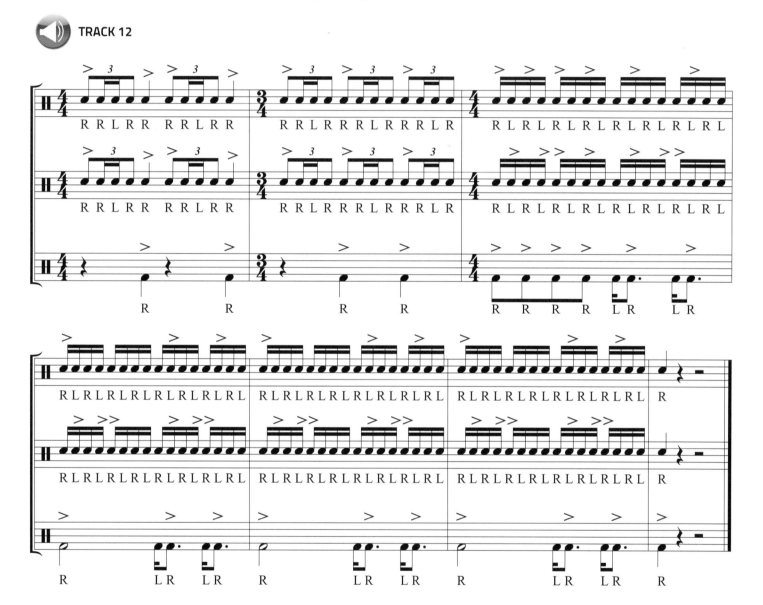

Now let's take a look at what Nação Porto Rico calls "chamada." The following chamada is usually played in the context of a song. For instance, the alfaias and caixas will stop playing during the verse of a song while the atabaques and agbês continue. Upon entering the bridge of the song there is sometimes a break where all of the instruments stop and the caixa plays the chamada, which is a four-beat pick-up, often times leading the group into the next section of the song.

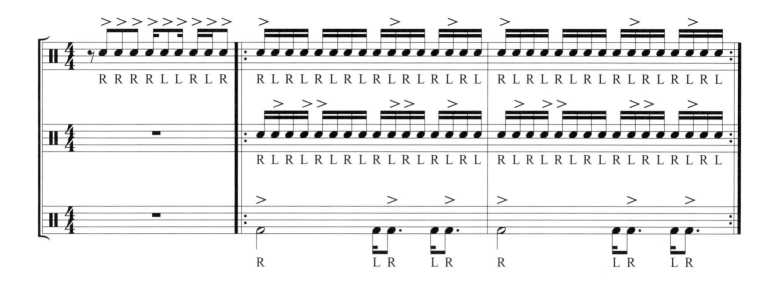

Atabaque Parts for Porto Rico

Here are a few examples of the atabaque parts played by Nação Porto Rico for Baque de Luanda. Mestre Shacon was the first one to add the atabaque to a traditional maracatu group. To this day, the atabaque instrument is still not widely used by other maracatu groups, though there are a few following Mestre Shacon's path, such as Nação Aurora Africana.

Break

TRACK 13
0:00–0:12

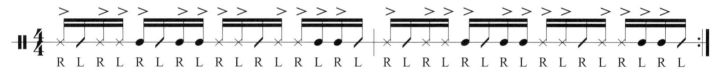

Baque de Luanda Variation 1

TRACK 13
0:13–0:26

Baque de Luanda Variation 2

TRACK 13
0:27–0:40

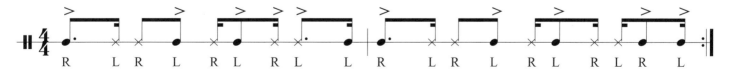

The following is a transcription of one of Mestre Shacon's songs, "Meu Baque é Lento." Notice how Porto Rico is always going in between a 6/8 and 4/4 feel with the atabaque.

TRACK 14

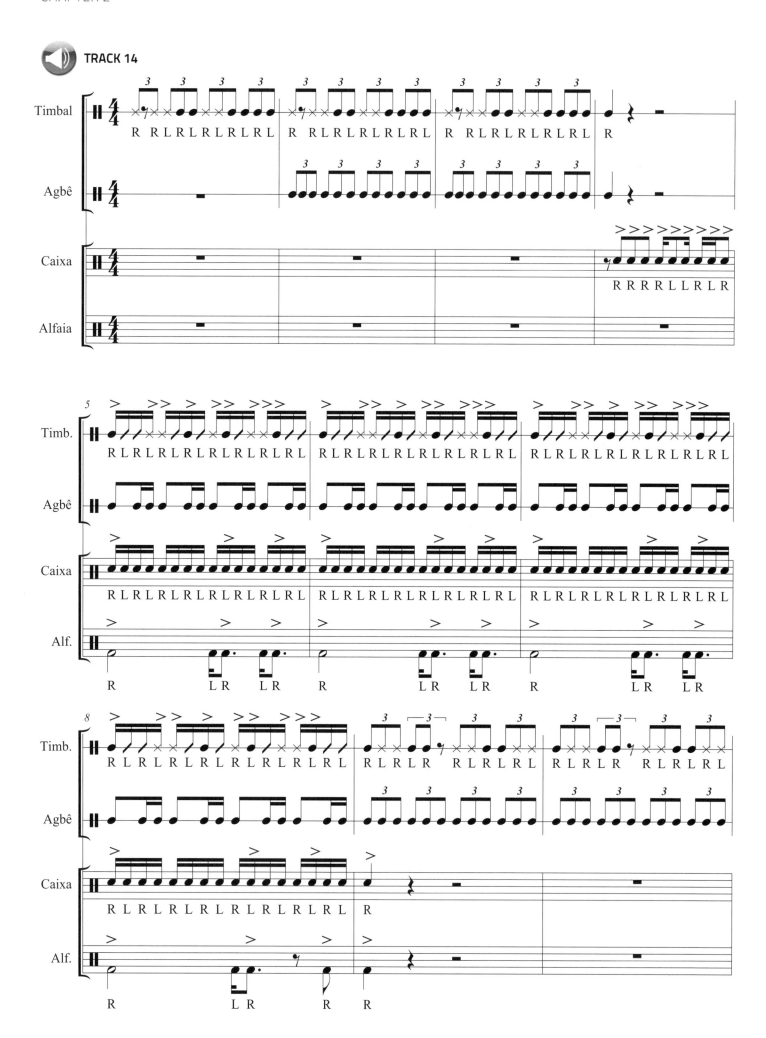

Nação Leão da Campina—Baque de Luanda

Leão da Campina Caixa

Leão da Campina Tarol

Tarol Variation 1

Tarol Variation 2

Tarol Variation 3

Leão da Campina Caixa Chamada: Baque de Luanda

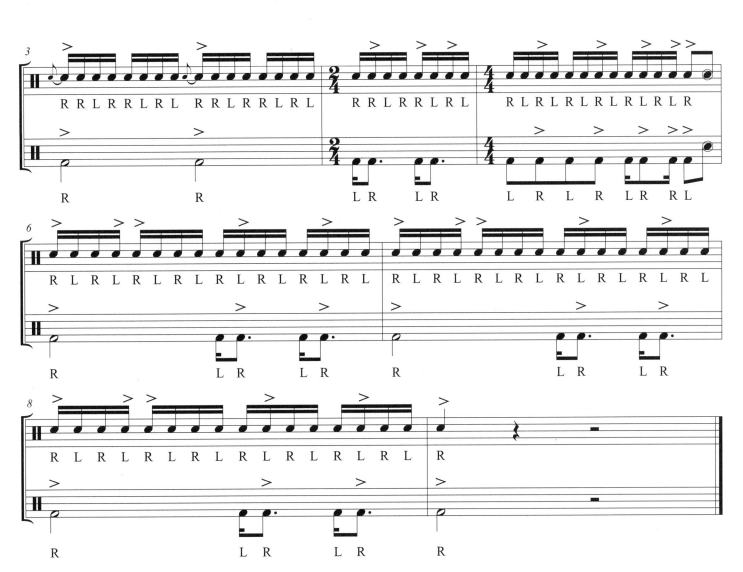

Chamada with all instruments in the style of Estrela Brilhante. Notice where the agbê, gonguê, and mineiro enter.

There is no metronome count-off in the following chamada example because there is an acceleration in tempo during the chamada. I've given you two stick clicks so you can prepare to play along with this track.

TRACK 15

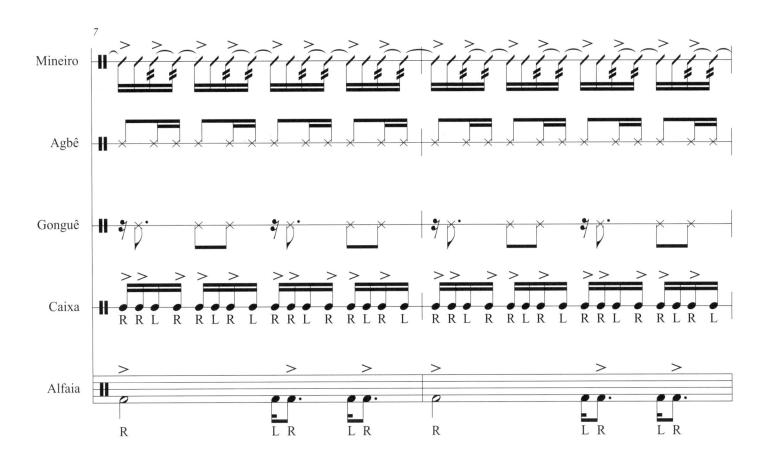

Drumset Examples

Now let's apply some of these rhythms to the drumset. The following exercises will help you develop your independence and dexterity around the drums. Be patient and start off at a slow tempo before moving on. It's important to internalize these feels and multiple polyrhythmic figures on the kit so that you can begin to add your own ideas on top of them and even create your own grooves based on these maracatu examples.

I can't emphasize enough the importance of studying all of the percussion material in this book and learning to play some of the percussion instruments before applying these rhythms to the drumset. Billy Hart always stressed to me that the drumset is a multi-percussion instrument constructed of different percussion instruments combined together. He always talked about how Baby Dodds, "Papa" Jo Jones, and most of the early drumset players considered themselves multi-percussionists. Having the knowledge of the percussion instruments used in maracatu and their technique will only enhance how well you play these rhythms on the drumset.

Let's start with a simple coordination exercise to get our feet working together. I like to put the gonguê pattern in the left foot with the hi-hat or a mounted cowbell and the alfaia parts in the bass drum. This can be complicated at first so be patient and start off slow. I also like to switch up the hi-hat pattern and just play the "ands" of the beat, which helps simplify the groove and gives a little more space for harmonic and melodic instruments to play on top of your groove.

Example A
These four combinations use the gonguê pattern in the left foot.

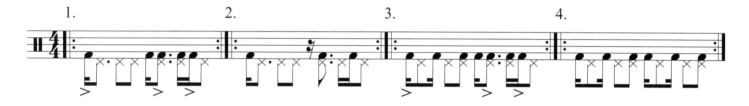

Example B
These four combinations use the hi-hat on the "ands" of the beat.

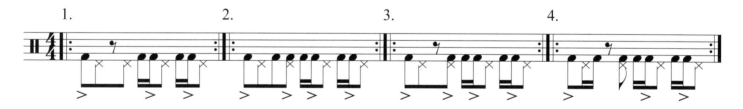

Example 1 starts off simply by orchestrating one of the basic caixa patterns on the snare drum and the alfaia part to the bass drum. Once you feel comfortable with example 1, move on to example 2 and add the gonguê pattern on the hi-hat.

Example 1

Example 2

 TRACK 16

Here are some drumset orchestration ideas using some of the caixa patterns from Estrela Brilhante. Don't forget to add the onguê pattern on the hi-hat with all of these grooves.

Example 3

Example 4

Example 5

Example 6

Now let's switch up the bass drum a little and play Baque de Imalê while playing some caixa patterns from Estrela Brilhante.

Example 7

 TRACK 17

Example 8

Example 9

 TRACK 18

Example 10

Here are a few examples using one of the caixa patterns from Leão da Campina.

Example 11

Example 12

Example 13

Example 14

TRACK 19

Now let's move the right hand to the ride cymbal while playing the RRLR–RLRL caixa pattern in the hands. We're not going to change anything except the sound source of our right hand by distributing our right hand to the ride cymbal. This is essentially how the drumset evolved in the early 20th century when New Orleans drummers began orchestrating rhythms around the drumkit for what used to be two or three percussionists. This is exactly what we are doing here. We'll talk about a lot more ideas of distributing our right hand using the RRLR–RLRL caixa pattern in a later chapter, but for now let's get started with this basic example.

Example 15

TRACK 20

Once you have a strong grasp on the above concept, try adding the onguê pattern to the left foot with the hi-hat.

Now let's try some of the Nação Porto Rico tarol parts on the drumset. Example 16 starts off simple by applying the tarol part directly to the snare drum. On examples 17 and 18 we will begin exploring some melodic ideas that can start to resemble a full maracatu group on the kit.

Example 16

TRACK 21
0:00–0:13

Example 17

TRACK 21
0:14–0:26

Example 18

TRACK 21
0:27–0:41

Once you feel comfortable with the previous examples, move your right hand to the ride cymbal and play a basic gonguê variation, which could also represent the agogô bell pattern. Play the following grooves on the shoulder and the bell of the ride while playing one of the feet combinations. This will free up your left hand to play the caixa parts and later improvise.

Example 19

TRACK 22
0:00–0:13

Example 20

TRACK 22
0:16-0:30

Example 21

Example 22

TRACK 23

Example 23

Example 24

Example 25

 TRACK 24

Maracatu Nação Estrela Brilhante practices in the streets in Alto Zé do Pinho. Recife, 2007.

Parading with Estrela Brilhante over the years and learning to play with their feel has helped me transfer these rhythms and feels to the drumset. I can't express enough how important it is for drumset players to learn to play the percussion instruments first.

Baque de Marcação Funk Ideas

Here are some ideas to apply maracatu in a funk context.

Example 1

 TRACK 25

Example 2: I like to use this one with my band Nation Beat. You can hear an example of this on the track "Nagô Nagô" on our album *Legends of the Preacher*.

Example 3

 TRACK 26
0:00–0:12

Example 4

 TRACK 26
0:13–0:25

Example 5

 TRACK 26
0:26–0:39

CHAPTER 3

Baque de Imalê

In this chapter we'll take a look at Baque de Imalê (pronounced ee-ma-LAY). After studying Baque de Marcação, you'll notice a very close relationship with these two rhythms. Imalê adds two eighth notes in the middle of the measure, which generates more energy and gives the groove a stronger sense of forward motion. Baque de Imalê can also lend itself to a strong funk feel. If you listen to Nação Estrela Brilhante de Igarassu you'll notice that the caixa plays a backbeat on top of the imalê groove in the alfaias.

Here's a list of some traditional maracatu groups that play Baque de Imalê, although they might play it with a slight variation.

- Maracatu Nação Estrela Brilhante
- Maracatu Nação Leão Coroado
- Maracatu Nação Cambinda Estrela
- Maracatu Nação Estrela Brilhante de Igarassu

Caixa Variations

Mestre Walter transcription: Baque de Imalê on the caixa

Here's a transcription of one of Mestre Walter's caixa parts for Baque de Imalê that he played for me during one of our lessons.

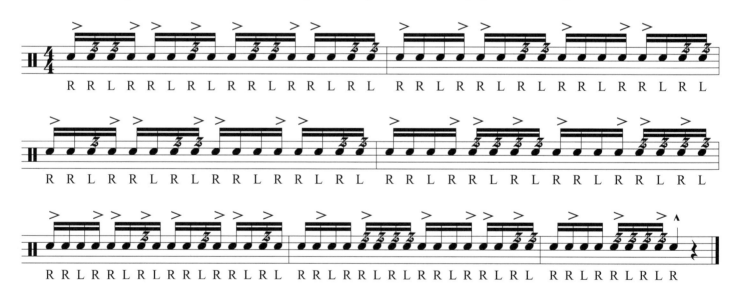

Baque de Imalê
Caixa Variation 1 (105 bpm)

 TRACK 27

Caixa Variation 2

Caixa Variation 3

Caixa variation 4 – Cambinda Estrela

 **TRACK 28**

Maracatu Nação Leão Coroado was founded in 1863. They are among the oldest maracatu groups in Recife who are still active and parading during Carnival every year. Mestre Luíz de França is one of the most popular maracatu mestres (leader of the percussion group) who led Leão Coroado from approximately 1954 through 1997. He took over the responsibilities of mestre after his father, an ex-slave and founder of Leão Coroado, passed the honor down to him.

Here are a couple examples of Leão Coroado caixa grooves for Baque de Imalê. They are known for playing at slower tempos, right around quarter note = 85 bpm. This makes their groove and swing really funky and almost dirge-like. They currently have a CD available called *140 Anos*. Try to find it online.

Nação Leão Coroado Variation 1 (85 bpm)

R L R L R L R L R L R L R L R L R L R L R L R L R L R L R L R L

Nação Leão Coroado Variation 2 (85 bpm)

 TRACK 29

R L R L R L R L R L R L R L R L R L R L R L R L R L R L R L R L

Alfaia Variations

Now let's take a look at some of the *basic* alfaia parts for Baque de Imalê. I stress the word "basic" because each group has many solo variations that some of the alfaias play on top of this groove. Sometimes the song inspires some of the alfaia players to improvise and fill in some of the gaps of the rhythm, but the examples below are what the marcante (low) alfaias would play for Baque de Imalê.

Here are a few examples of Baque de Imalê played by three different groups: Nação Estrela Brilhante, Nação Leão Coroado, and Nação Estrela Brilhante de Igarassu. Pay close attention to the similarities and the nuanced differences.

Baque de Imalê – Estrela Brilhante (105 bpm)

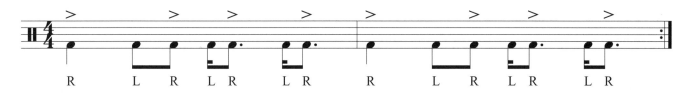

R   L R L R   L R   R   L R L R   L R

Baque de Imalê – Leão Coroardo (85 bpm)

 TRACK 30

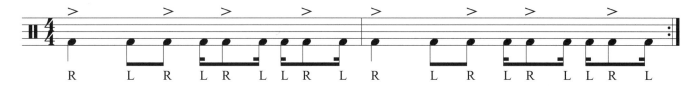

R   L R L R L L R L R   L R L R L L R L

Baque de Imalê – Cambinda Estrela. Notice that this is very similar to Estrela Brilhante, only here Cambinda leaves out a sixteenth note on beat three. (105 bpm)

Baque de Imalê – Estrela Brilhante de Igarassu (110 bpm)

 TRACK 31

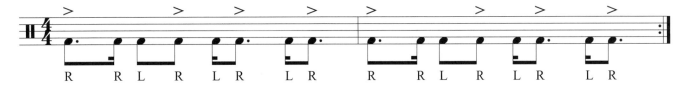

Note: Estrela Brilhante de Igarassu plays with a heavy wood mallet in the strong hand and a small twig in the left hand, just like Porto Rico. This not only helps accentuate the accent in the strong hand, but the twig produces a slap sound against the skin that makes their sound unique from other maracatu groups. I recommend experimenting playing this groove the same way so you really get a sense of the sound and how this changes the overall sonic impact of this groove.

Maracatu Nação Leão Coroado Variation on Baque de Imalê (85 bpm)

 TRACK 32

Maracatu Nação Estrela Brilhante variation on Baque de Imalê (105 bpm)

This is an example of how Estrela Brilhante played their chamada to the "Evolução de Bateria" track from their self-titled CD.

🔊 TRACK 33

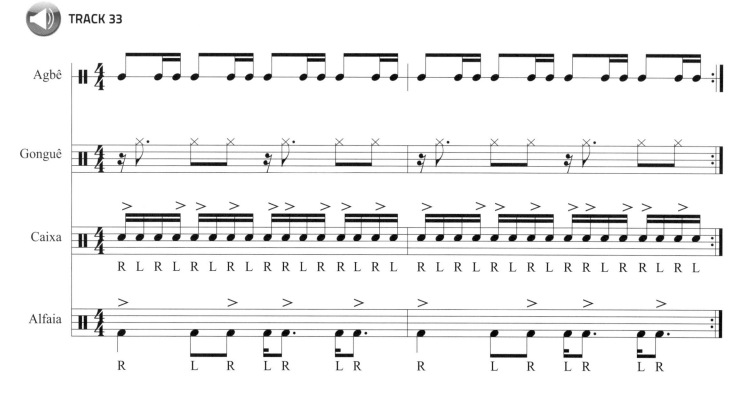

Here's a score view of Baque de Imalê with the caixa chamada. Remember to keep the tempo loose in the beginning and gradually accelerate in the first few measures. Don't count yourself off, even if you're playing with other caixa players. Use body language to start everyone off at the same time.

This is how Estrela Brilhante plays "Evolução de Bateria" on their CD. Notice how the instruments enter differently.

There is no metronome count-off in the following chamada example because there is an acceleration in tempo during the chamada. I've given you two stick clicks so you can prepare to play along with this track.

Baque de Imalê with Chamada

🔊 TRACK 34

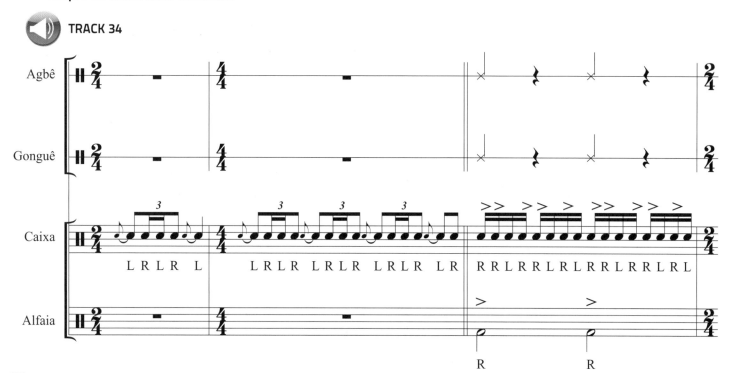

Parading with Big Chief Monk Boudreaux on Mardi Gras day. Monk loved hearing the maracatu rhythms behind his chants and immediately noticed the similarities between the Mardi Gras Indian and maracatu rhythms such as Baque de Martelo. Photo by Danielle Maia Cruz, 2012.

CHAPTER 4

Baque de Martelo

"Beat of the Hammer"—that's the literal translation for this groove. Baque de Martelo is probably the least commonly heard groove played by the traditional maracatu groups in Recife and the most unique. It has very little similarities to all of the other grooves most commonly heard by other maracatu groups. Nação Estrela Brilhante, Nação Porto Rico, Nação Cambinda Estrela, and Nação Encanto da Alegria are among the traditional groups who use Baque de Martelo.

For an example of Baque de Martelo you can download "Somos de Água Fria" by Maracatu New York or Nation Beat featuring Nação Estrela Brilhante. You can also try to find "Vou Buscar Ramos Verdes" by Nação Encanto da Alegria, "Águas Verdes" by Nação Porto Rico, and "Nós Somos Cambinda Estrela" by Nação Cambinda Estrela.

Groups who play Baque de Martelo:

- Nação Estrela Brilhante
- Nação Porto Rico
- Nação Cambinda Estrela
- Nação Encanto da Alegria

Caixa Variations

Check out some of these caixa patterns. You'll notice that this caixa pattern is very similar to Baque de Marcação. However pay close attention to the accent variations; they tend to be slightly different for this groove.

Baque de Martelo Basic Caixa Pattern: similar to Baque de Marcação

R R L R R L R L R R L R R L R L   R R L R R L R L R R L R R L R L

Baque de Martelo Caixa Variation 1

R R L R R L R L R R L R R   R R L R R L R L R R L R R

Baque de Martelo Caixa Variation 2 (100 bpm)

🔊 TRACK 35

R R L R R L R L R R L R R   L   R R L R R L R L R R L R R   L

Baque de Martelo Caixa Variation 3

R R L R R L R L R R L R R L R L   R R L R R L R L R R L R R L R L

Baque de Martelo Caixa Variation 4

R R L R R L R L R R L R R L R L   R R L R R L R L R R L R R L R L

Mestre Walter Caixa Variation

This is a transcription of one of the examples that Mestre Walter played for me during a lesson at his house.

R R L R R L R L R R L R R L R L   R R L R R L R L R R L R R L R L

R R L R R L R L R R L R R L R L   R R L R R L R L R R L R R L R L

R R L R R L R L R R L R R L R L   R R L R R L R L   L R L R

Alfaia Variations

The alfaia parts for Baque de Martelo really define this groove and make it unique from the other maracatu grooves. Be sure that your accents are strong and the unaccented notes are very soft to help make this groove really pop. Also notice that this groove starts off with the weak hand, whereas every other groove starts with the strong hand.

Baque de Martelo Basic Alfaia Pattern (100 bpm)

TRACK 36
0:00–0:22

L R R L R L R R L   L R R L R L R R L   L R R L R L R R L   L R R L R L R R L

TRACK 36
0:23-0:45

Baque de Martelo Alfaia Variation 1

Baque de Martelo Alfaia Variation 2 – Nação Porto Rico

Estrela Brilhante: Martelo Break with Caixa

TRACK 37

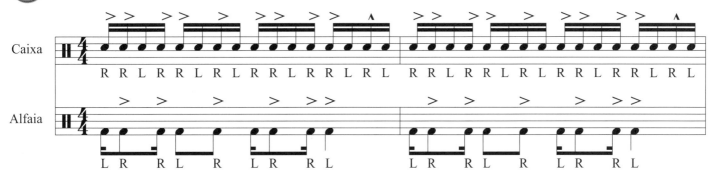

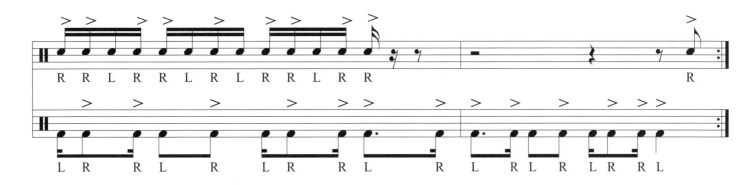

Here are three alfaia parts for Baque de Martelo played by Nação Estrela Brilhante that I learned in 2001 when I was living in Recife. It's rare to hear them playing these parts today, but you'll still often find a few members of the group playing these parts.

 TRACK 38

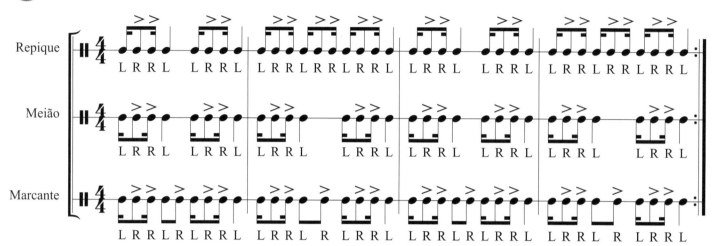

Baque de Martelo with Chamada

Pay very close attention to this chamada. You'll notice that it starts off exactly the same as every other chamada; however, it gets cut in half and the groove starts on bar 4.

There is no metronome count-off in the following chamada example because there is an acceleration in tempo during the chamada. I've given you two stick clicks so you can prepare to play along with this track.

 **TRACK 39**

Nação Cambinda Estrela Baque de Martelo Variation with Chamada: Here's another variation to check out. Notice how different this groove feels by leaving out one sixteenth note on beat three.

There is no metronome count-off in the following chamada example because there is an acceleration in tempo during the chamada. I've given you two stick clicks so you can prepare to play along with this track.

 TRACK 40

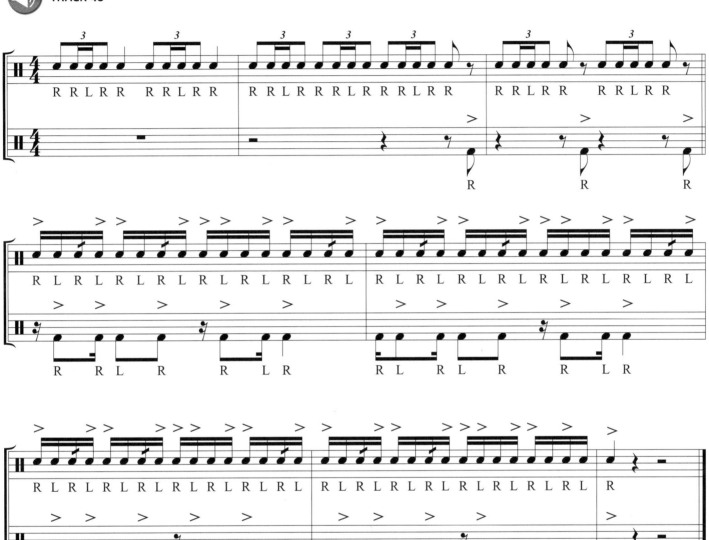

CHAPTER 5

Baque de Arrasto

Baque de Arrasto is a groove most commonly played by Nação Estrela Brilhante and Nação Encanto da Alegria. For me, this groove really embodies the essence of all the maracatu rhythms. Baque de Arrasto has a constant sense of flipping over and over again without giving a strong emphasis on the downbeat. It's easy to get lost inside of this groove, so be careful not to rush and always listen to the gonguê to know exactly where you are in the beat.

For examples you can check out "Roda Baiana" by Nação Encanto da Alegria and recorded by Maracatu New York, and "Dança Rainha" by Nação Estrela Brilhante.

Caixa Variations

Baque de Arrasto Caixa Variation 1: Estrela Brilhante (98 bpm)

 TRACK 41

Baque de Arrasto Caixa Variation 2: Encanto da Alegria

 TRACK 42

Alfaia Variations

The alfaia part for Baque de Arrasto is generally played the same by each group who uses this rhythm. Pay very close attention to the accents and be careful not to rush.

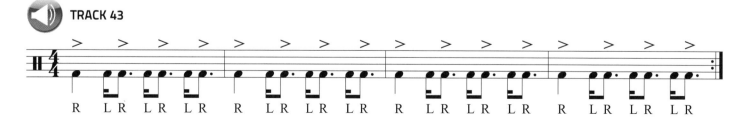 TRACK 43

Baque de Arrasto with Chamada

Here's one example of how Encanto da Alegria plays a chamada. Check out Roda Baiana from their CD *Baque Forte*.

There is no metronome count-off in the following chamada example because there is an acceleration in tempo during the chamada. I've given you two stick clicks so you can prepare to play along with this track.

TRACK 44

CHAPTER 6

Alfaia Variations

Convenções—Bridge Variations

I prefer calling the convenção (convention) a bridge since the word "convention" has no musical reference. Convenções are variations that take place within each baque that help delineate the form of the song or transition to another section in the song or arrangement. Each nação has its own variations; however, these are the most commonly heard variations from the traditional maracatu groups in Recife. Again, pay close attention to the sticking and accents as these help shape the feel and swing of the groove.

Basic Convenção – Bridge 1

TRACK 45
0:00–0:10

R L R L R R L R R   R L R L R R L R R

Bridge 2

This variation is similar to the previous one; however, notice the end of the phrase is different.

TRACK 45
0:11–0:22

R L R L R R L R L R   R L R L R R L R L R

Bridge 3

This convenção is often played by Estrela Brilhante. Notice how the phrase goes over the barline.

TRACK 45
0:23–0:29

R L R L R R L R L R R L   R L R L R R L R L R R L

Leão Coroado Bridge

R L R L R L L R L   R L R L R L L R L   R L R L R L L R L   R R R R L R L L R L

Parada Variations

In Portuguese, "parada" means "stop." These are just a few paradas that you will often hear being played by some of the traditional maracatu groups in Recife. It is very important that you learn all of these, as they will be applied in the following chapter for Baque de Parada. These parada variations can be used in many different contexts. You can use these variations as a parade beat, looping the parada over and over while parading down a street that doesn't have many onlookers, or as part of an arrangement. You can also use them to create a tension/release; looping the parada creates a tension, and then you can release it into a baque such as Baque de Imalê. These parada variations will also be used in Baque de Parada, as discussed in the following chapter.

Parada Variation 1 – Nação Estrela Brilhante (105 bpm)

 **TRACK 46**

R   R L R   R L R   R L   R   R   R   R L R   R L R   R L   R   R

Parada Variation 2 – Nação Estrela Brilhante

R   R L R   R L R   R L   R L   R   R   R L R   R L R   R L   R L   R

Parada Variation 3 – Nação Porto Rico (98 bpm)

 TRACK 47

R   R L R   R   R   R L   R L R   R L   R   R

Parada Variation 4 – Nação Cambinda Estrela (105 bpm)

 **TRACK 48**

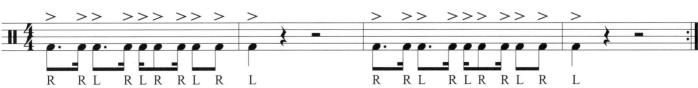

R   R L   R L R   R L   R   L   R   R L   R L R   R L   R   L

Parada—Bridge

This exercise will help you transition smoothly from the parada to the bridge. This is a very important exercise because you will need to play this transition a lot when playing with a maracatu group.

Variation 1 (105 bpm)

 TRACK 49

Variation 2 (105 bpm)

Nação Aurora Africana

Parada Variation 1

Check out this parada groove that is played by Aurora Africana. (119 bpm)

 TRACK 50

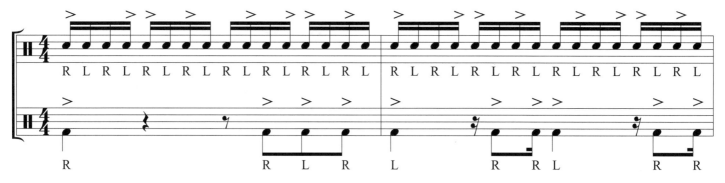

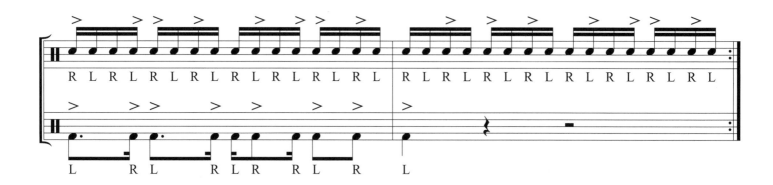

Parada Variation 2

Here is another parada groove that is played by Aurora Africana. Notice that the 2nd and 3rd endings are on cue. This means that the first ending will repeat until the mestre blows the whistle and sends the cue for the 2nd or 3rd ending.

TRACK 51

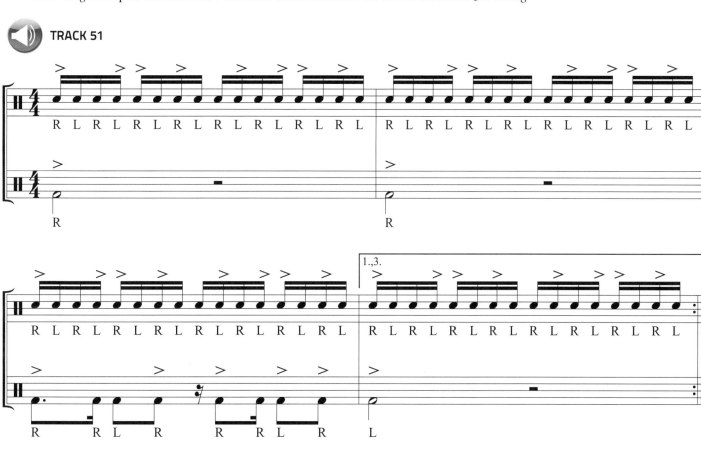

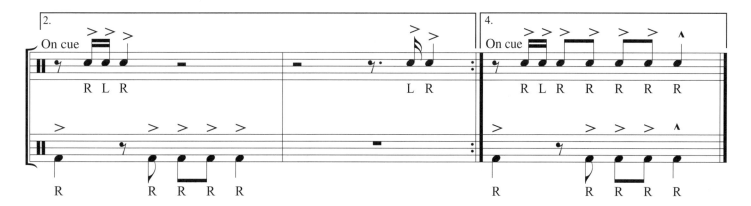

Bridge—Parada

This exercise will help you transition smoothly from the bridge to the parada. Again, this is a very common transition, so you'll want to spend a lot of time internalizing these examples.

Variation 1

TRACK 52
0:00-0:15

Variation 2

TRACK 52
0:16-0:30

Baque de Marcação with Bridge

Here are a few examples of playing Baque de Marcação with the bridge on every fourth measure. Practice this exercise with a metronome at a slow tempo until you can make these transitions between the baque (groove) and the bridge smoothly. Once you feel comfortable with all of these transitions, start to move the tempo up and practice improvising in between the bridge variations instead of playing the baque.

Bridge 1

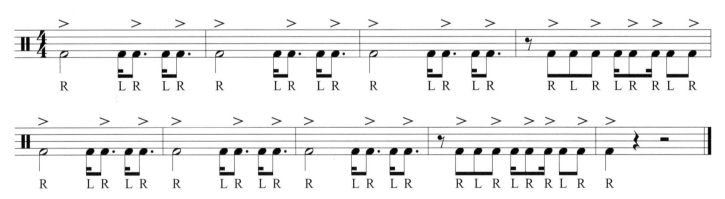

Bridge 2

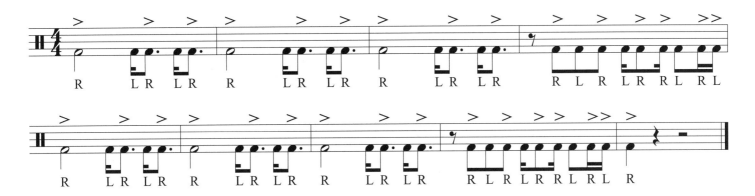

Bridge 3

Pay close attention to this bridge variation. It's very similar to the previous bridge; however, take note of how the bridge pattern goes over the barline on measure 5. This is a bridge pattern often played by Nação Estrela Brilhante.

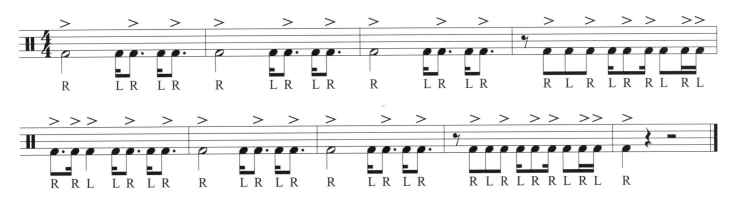

Bridge 4

Here's another really cool bridge variation, also played by Nação Estrela Brilhante. You can hear Estrela play this bridge with Nation Beat on the song "Clementina de Jesus no Morro da Conceição."

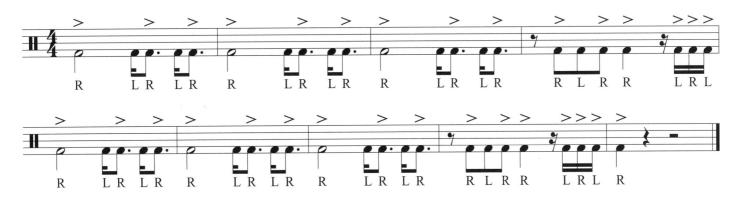

This is a combination of the two previous bridge patterns playing over the barline on measure 5. I first heard Mestre Walter using this bridge with Estrela Brilhante in 2003. They recorded this bridge on the Nation Beat CD *Maracatuniversal* on the track "Clementina de Jesus No Morro da Conceição."

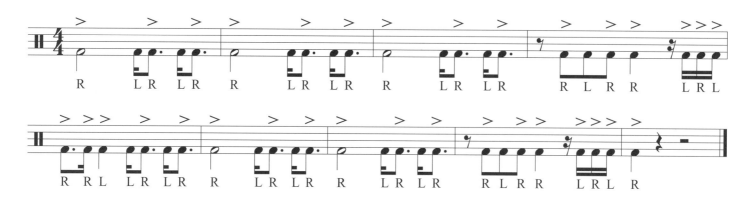

Mestre Walter from Maracatu Nação Estrela Brilhante showing Scott Kettner some tips on how to play maracatu on the drumset during the recording of *Maracatuniversal* in Recife, Brazil with Nation Beat, 2005.

CHAPTER 7

Baque de Parada

Baque de Parada (The Stopping Beat) is a very common groove among the traditional maracatu groups in Recife. As you'll notice in this chapter, there are many variations for playing Baque de Parada, and these are only some of them! It is very important that you have a solid understanding of Baque de Marcação, Baque de Imalê, and Baque de Arrasto, since these grooves make up the foundation for Baque de Parada.

For an example of Baque de Parada, check out the song "Dança Rainha" by Nação Estrela Brilhante or "Nagô Nagô" by Nação Porto Rico. Notice how the forms of these songs are completely different. This is a perfect example of how diverse each traditional maracatu group and their grooves are from one another. On "Dança Rainha," the Baque de Parada form is very long, whereas on "Nagô Nagô" the form is much shorter. These forms are dictated by the melody and the lyrics. That's why it is very important to learn the melody and the lyrics and practice playing and singing at the same time. This goes for any style of music that you play.

Baque de Parada Variation 1: Note that this version of Baque de Parada combines Baque de Marcação and Parada. The entire cycle played repeatedly forms the groove, Baque de Parada. There are many variations of Baque de Parada depending on the nação and the arrangement. In this version I used baque de marcação, but you can use Imalê or Arrasto for the first three measures (track 18). 105 bpm

🔊 **TRACK 53**

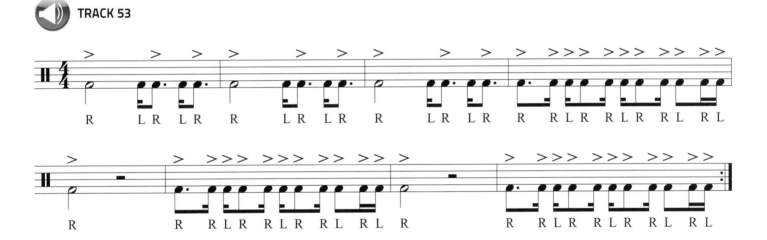

Baque de Parada Variation 2: This version of Baque de Parada is the same as the previous version except the bridge pattern is added onto the end, forming a 9-bar cycle. The entire cycle played repeatedly forms the Baque de Parada. Again, this version uses baque de marcação.

TRACK 54

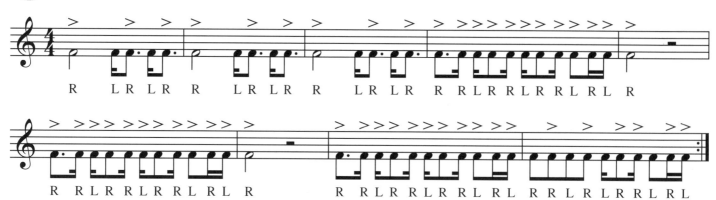

Baque de Parada Variation 3: Now let's play Baque de Parada using imalê in the alfaia.

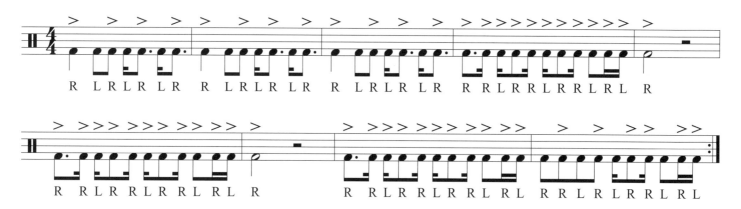

Baque de Parada Variation 4: Now let's play Baque de Parada using arrasto in the alfaia.

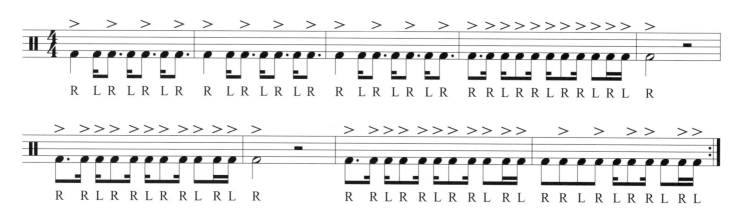

Baque de Parada with Chamada Using Arrasto

Here's a variation on Baque de Parada using arrasto. This is an example of how Estrela Brilhante might play Baque de Parada. Notice the sticking variations on the caixa part.

Levante a Bandeira, by Mestre Walter and Éder "O" Rocha.

Check out the Baque de Parada form on this track by Nação Estrela Brilhante. This is a very unique form of Baque de Parada because of the use of the 2/4 measure. This is the foundation of what the marcante alfaias play on this track. You'll notice that on the second time through the song, the meião alfaias begin to solo on top; however, this form is always intact. You'll also notice that every time Mestre Walter sings "Com Baque Parada e o Baque Trovão," the alfaias play the parada pattern.

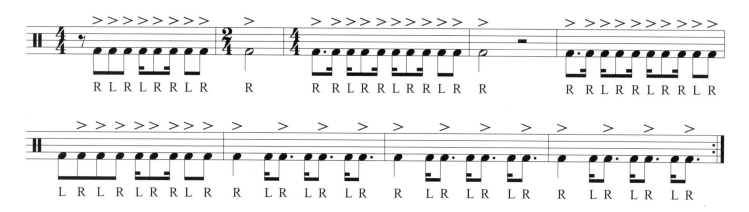

Baque de Parada – Nação Cambinda Estrela

This is also a very unique way of playing Baque de Parada. On this version, Cambinda Estrela plays it as an instrumental. You'll notice they are using Baque de Imalê as seen in Chapter 3. Check out how they end their parada phrase on the left hand with an accent. Make sure you are able to get your left hand as loud as your right hand for instances like these.

 TRACK 55

Leão da Campina

Baque Parado Caixa

Nação Leão da Campina calls this Baque Parado instead of Baque de Parada.

Parado 1

Parado 2

Baque Parado – as played by Leão da Campina

 TRACK 56

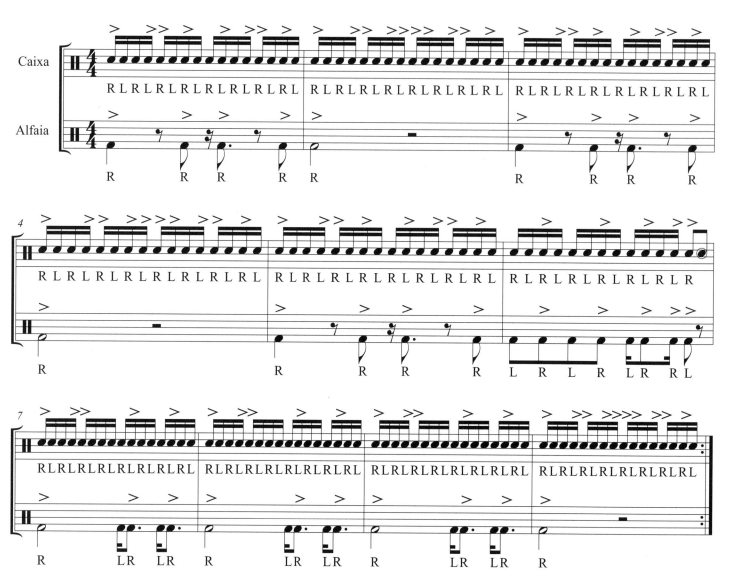

Baque Misto

Leão da Campina calls this Baque de Malê instead of Imalê, though they are the same groove.

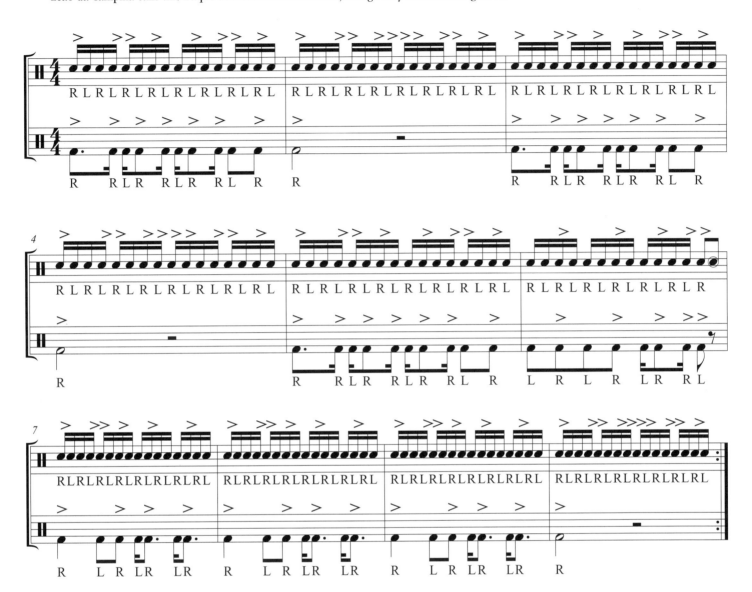

CHAPTER 8

Additional Chamadas

This section will explore some of the additional chamada variations from various traditional maracatu groups. We'll also explore some contemporary chamadas that I came up with based on the traditional chamadas for my group, Maracatu New York. In this section we'll only look at the caixa and alfaia parts. I encourage you to find these chamadas on either YouTube or some other source and learn the bell and shaker parts on your own. It's important to maintain the oral aspect of learning this music, and there's nothing more rewarding than finding new material on your own.

There is no metronome count-off in the following chamada example because there is an acceleration in tempo during the chamada. I've given you two stick clicks so you can prepare to play along with this track.

Cambinda Estrela

TRACK 57

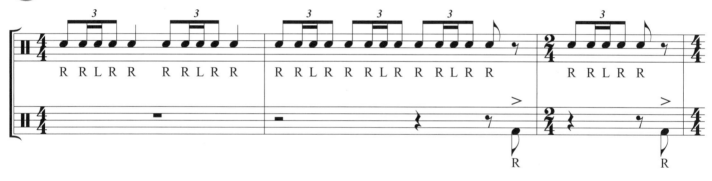

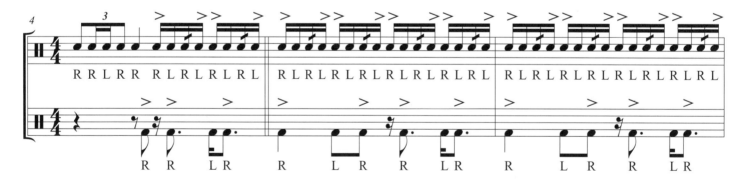

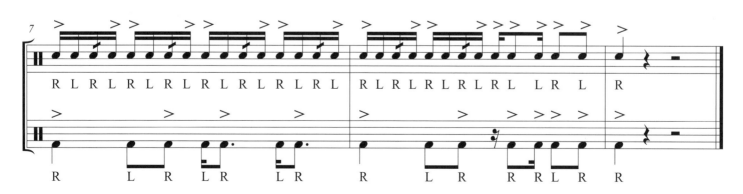

Nação Encanto da Alegria

There is no metronome count-off in the following chamada example because there is an acceleration in tempo during the chamada. I've given you two stick clicks so you can prepare to play along with this track.

Nação Porto Rico

 TRACK 58

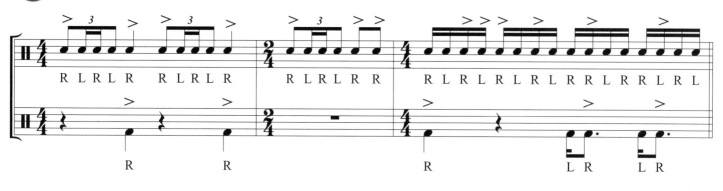

Maracatu New York

Baque de Brooklyn performed by Maracatu New York.

Here's a full track called "Baque de Brooklyn" (the beat of Brooklyn) from my group Maracatu New York. I've included a transcription of just the chamada on this track so you can check it out and learn it. There's no count-off since this is a full performance from our latest CD, *Baque do Brooklyn*. Listen to the entire track to see how I've incorporated the traditional baques from previous chapters in this book as well as some of the solo patterns discussed later on.

 TRACK 59

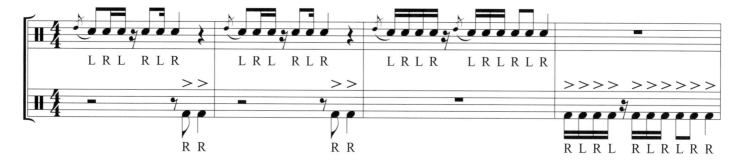

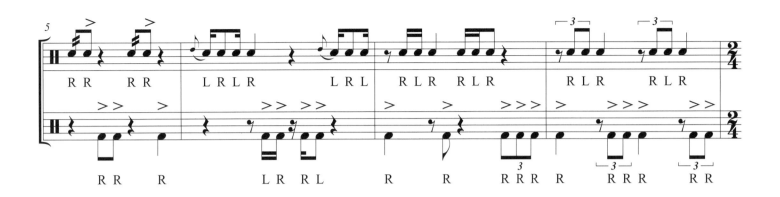

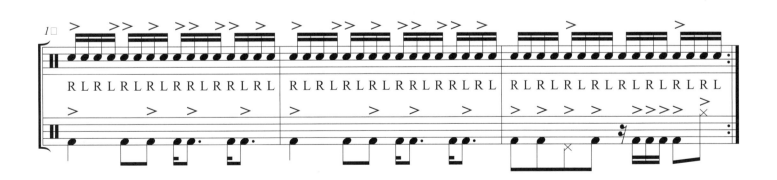

CHAPTER 9

Virar—Solo Patterns for Alfaia

In Portuguese, "virar" means to flip. To "virar" refers to the rhythmic illusion of flipping the beat over and over again. These are solo patterns that are unique to each group. It's impossible to write down every variation from any group, since each time it's played it could be slightly different. However, these basic virar patterns will help you understand the foundation and the rhythmic concept for soloing on the alfaia in the context of playing Maracatu de Baque Virado.

Solo Variation 1: Notice that this solo pattern starts with the right hand and continues to "flip" starting with the left hand on the continuous measures.

TRACK 60
0:00–0:12

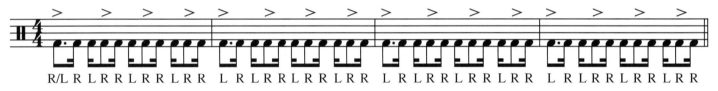

R/L R L R R L R R L R R   L R L R R L R R L R R   L R L R R L R R L R R   L R L R R L R R L R R

Solo Variation 2

TRACK 60
0:13–0:26

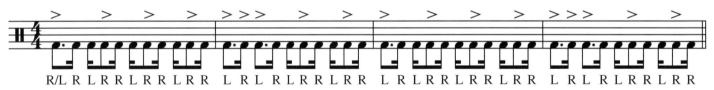

R/L R L R R L R R L R R   L R L R R L R R L R R   L R L R R L R R L R R   L R L R R L R R L R R

Solo Variation 3: This is a combinations of variations 1 and 2 using the bridge at the end of each 4-bar phrase.

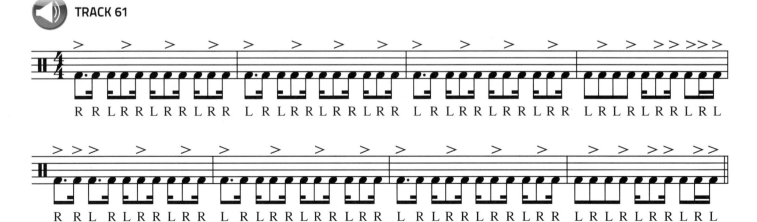
TRACK 61

R R L R R L R R L R R   L R L R R L R R L R R   L R L R R L R R L R R   L R L R L R R L R L

R R L R L R R L R R   L R L R R L R R L R R   L R L R R L R R L R R   L R L R L R R L R L

Solo Variation 4

 TRACK 62

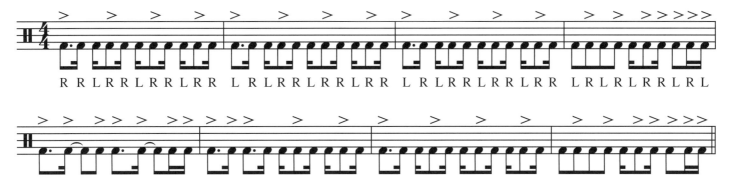

Solo Variation 5

 TRACK 63

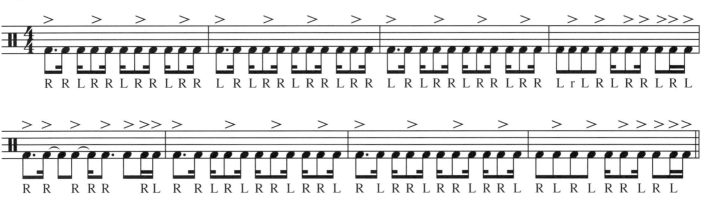

Solo Variation 6: This is another example of a solo pattern played by Aurora Africana.

Nação Porto Rico Solo Variations

Solo Variation 1: Nação Porto Rico

TRACK 64

Solo Variation 2: Nação Porto Rico. Here's a solo I transcribed from Mestre Shacon that he played for me during our interview. This is an example of the Yan Marcado alfaia part. Remember that Nação Porto Rico has four alfaia parts: the biancó, melê, yan, and yandarrum. All of these drums have a specific function and always solo together, which helps create the sophisticated melodic parts in the alfaias of Nação Porto Rico.

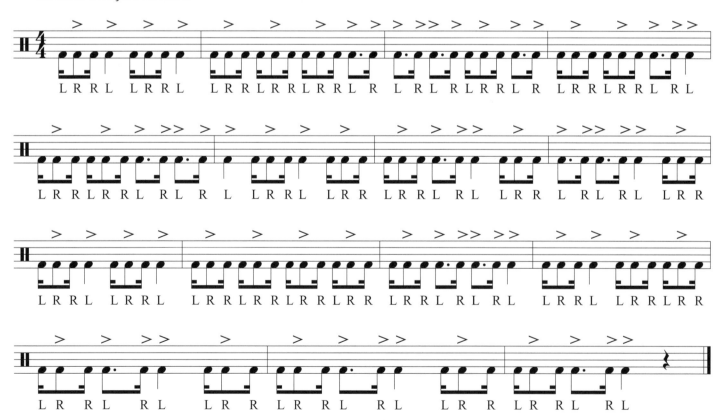

Biancó, Melê, and Yan Alfaias

Pay very close attention to how these three alfaia parts interact with each other. This conversation between the alfaias is one of the aspects that defines the sound and complexity of Nação Porto Rico. There are many different variations on this example; however, this is one of the most frequently played solos by Porto Rico and will help give you an insight to their style. Try practicing this example together with a few friends playing the caixa or tarol and all of the alfaia parts so you can get a good idea of how these parts work together.

A reminder that Porto Rico offers classes every week from their headquarters in Pina, which is located in Recife, Pernambuco, in case you have the opportunity to travel there and learn more about these rhythms directly from the source. You can find their contact info in the back of this book.

TRACK 65

Estrela Brilhante: three alfaia solo variations played together

TRACK 66

Repique—Solo Patterns

The "repique" refers to the smallest/highest pitched alfaia in Maracatu Nação Estrela Brilhante. The repiques play the pattern continuously throughout the song when the mestre gives the signal to start. They stop playing this pattern either when the song ends or when the mestre gives the signal to stop. Mestre Walter explains the repique as being the cousin to the caixa; they pratically play the same part. There are many different repique patterns and sticking variations. Here are two repique variations to get you started.

Repique 1: Baque de Marcação

TRACK 67
0:00-0:12

Repique 2: Baque de Imalê

TRACK 67
0:13-0:24

Baque Impulso—Estrela Brilhante

Mestre Walter is always creating new arrangements, new songs and new breaks. He caught me off guard in our interview about this one. He calls this Baque Impulso (impulse beat). What he's really referring to is the high-pitched alfaia or the repique. This is essentially a Baque de Imalê groove with the meião alfaia playing a solo—or as Mestre Walter calls it, "dobrando"—the repique playing Baque Impulso, and the marcante playing Imalê. The part that makes this Baque Impulso are the two eighth notes at the end of every second measure. Walter emphasized that these eighth-note turnarounds are what makes this Baque Impulso.

TRACK 68

In my interview with Mestre Walter, he explained how he divides the alfaias into groups by sizes:

Tambores 75cm–85cm: Play Imalê. These would be the Marcantes.

Tambores 65cm: Dobrando. Meião.

Tambores 45cm–55cm: Play the Impulso. Repique.

Solo Variation 9: Nação Leão Coroado, three alfaia solo variations played together.

 TRACK 69

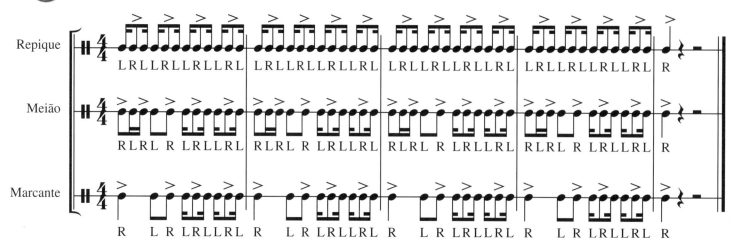

Solo Variation 10: Nação Leão Coroado, three alfaia solo variations played together.

 TRACK 70

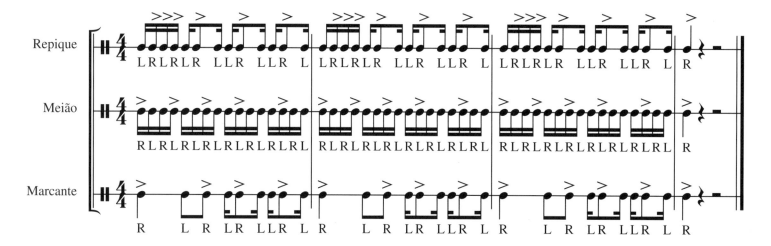

Baque de Parada—Nação Aurora Africana Using Imalê

Check out this Imalê groove with the meião alfaias playing a solo variation while the marcante alfaias maintain the Imalê groove.

 TRACK 71

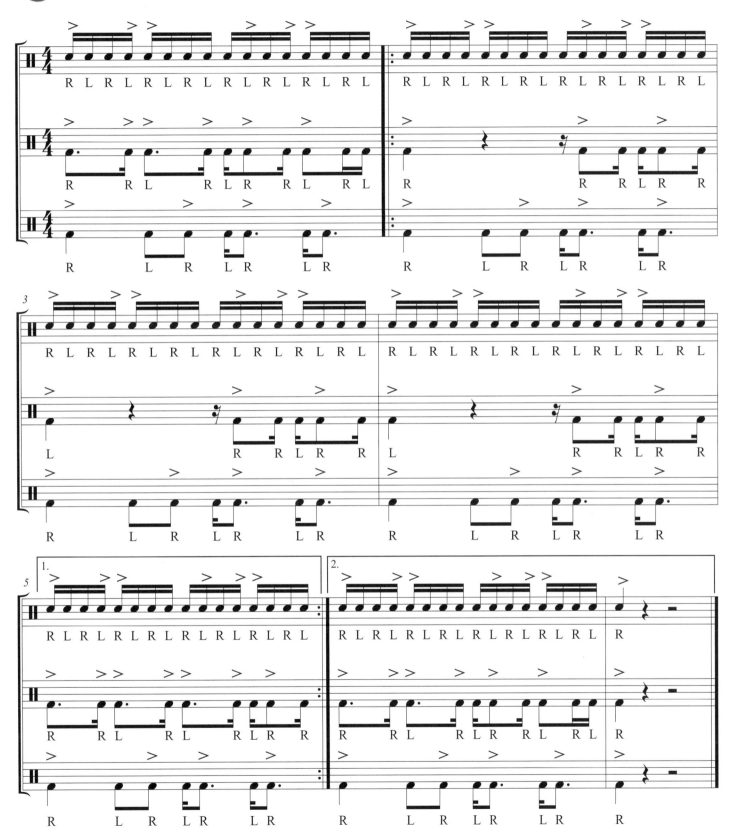

Baque de Parada Variation 2—Nação Aurora Africana Using Imalê

 TRACK 72

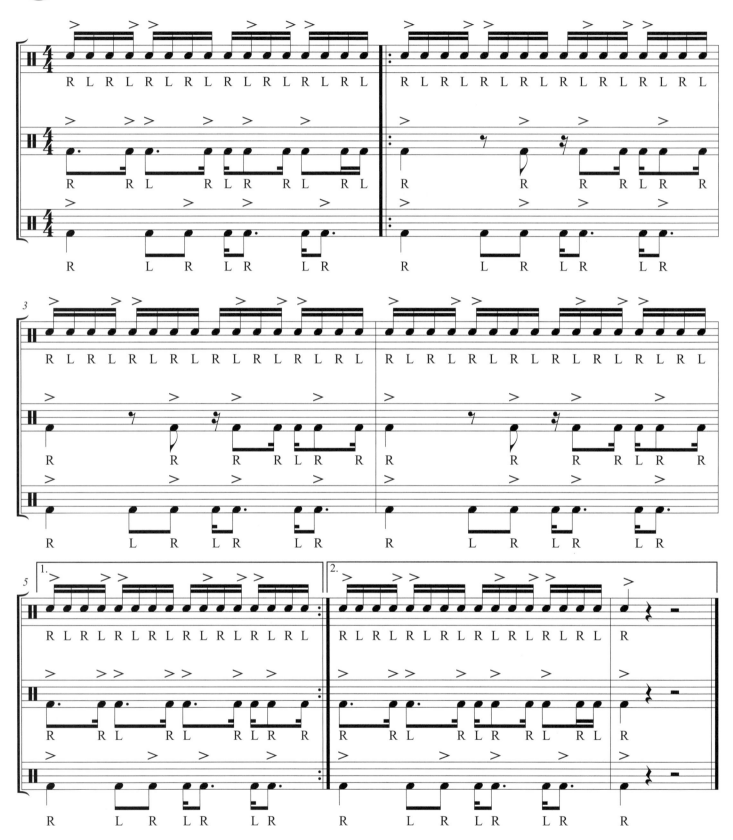

CHAPTER 10

Chico Science—Mangue Beat Grooves

As discussed on page 24 in the Contemporary Maracatu Manifestations section of this book, Chico Science was an innovative musician who creatively fused together the sound of heavy rock and funk music with maracatu and other folkloric rhythms from Recife. He is largely responsible for the resurgence and popularity of the traditional maracatu groups in Recife. It's impossible to discuss maracatu without mentioning Chico Science and the importance of the Mangue Beat Movement. Here are some examples of grooves from Chico's albums *Da Lama ao Caos* and *Afrociberdelia* that will help give you an insight on how he morphed traditional maracatu rhythms into contemporary funk grooves without losing the essence of the maracatu feel.

Da Lama ao Caos (102 bpm)

TRACK 73
0:00–0:12

A Cidade (96 bpm)

TRACK 73
0:14–0:38

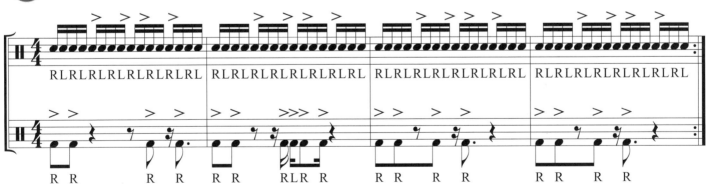

Um Passeio No Mundo Livre (96 bpm)

TRACK 73
0:39-1:03

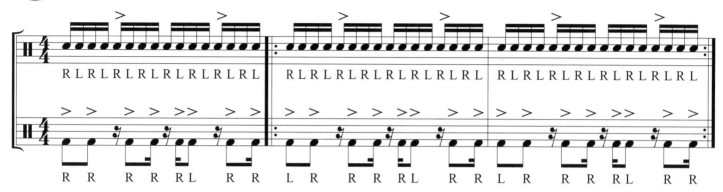

Etnia (102 bpm)

TRACK 73
1:05-1:28

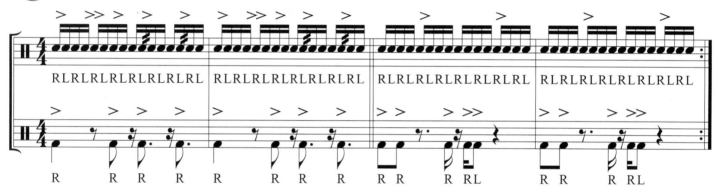

O Cidadão do Mundo (96 bpm)

TRACK 73
1:29-1:43

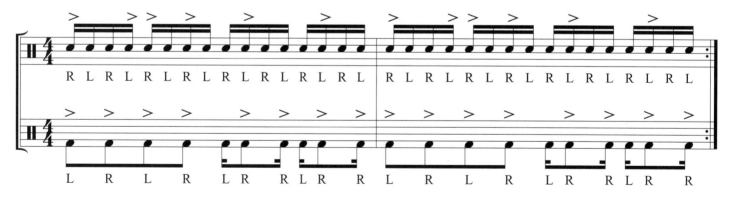

Da Lama ao Caos Groove Ideas for Drumset

Here are some fun grooves I came up with after deconstructing the groove played on *Da Lama ao Caos* and reconstructing it on the drumset. I've tried to maintain the essence of the groove in each example without changing the rhythm by displacing the notes from the bass drum to the snare drum.

You'll notice a striking similarity here to a lot of the grooves Jabo Starks played with James Brown, as mentioned in the Mangue Beat historical section of this book, when Maureliano helped come up with the main groove for Chico Science using the horn lines and grooves by the James Brown band. (102 bpm)

Example 1

Example 2

Example 3

Example 4

Example 5

Example 6

Drum maker Maureliano Ribeiro builds an alfaia out of macaiba in his workshop, (2011). Maureliano used James Brown as his main influence when helping Chico Science create the grooves for Nação Zumbi.

CHAPTER 11

From the Mississippi to the Capibaribe
Morphing Brazil with New Orleans on the Drumset

RRLR–RLRL

RRLR–RLRL was the first maracatu caixa pattern that I learned on my first trip to Recife when Larry Crook introduced me to Jorge Martins. This was the foundation for me to learn infinite variations on the maracatu caixa. As I continued to get deeper into playing and studying maracatu, I also noticed a lot of similarities with New Orleans Second Line and Mardi Gras Indian rhythms. Needless to say I wasn't surprised when I discovered Stanton Moore's book on New Orleans rhythms, *Take it To The Street*. In this book he discusses the RRLR–RLRL snare drum patterns used by the Mardi Gras Indians and Second Line drummers.

Looking back on the history of slave trade in New Orleans and Recife, I noticed a lot of the slaves brought to these two cities came from Angola and the Congo. They brought with them their rituals, culture, rhythms, and song and dance. New Orleans had Congo Square, a market place where slaves gathered and performed and danced on Sundays, and Recife had Nossa Senhora dos Homens Pretos, the church where slaves gathered and the maracatu crowning ceremonies took place with the celebration of drumming. These two meeting places where slaves were able to gather and play their instruments gave birth to many unique hybrids and manifestations of music and culture in both cities. It should come to no surprise that after hundreds of years many of these elements and their distant cousins remain intact still to this day.

The Capibaribe is a famous river that runs through the city of Recife. This chapter will explore some ideas on bringing together the distant rhythmic cousins of Recife and New Orleans on the drumset by joining the Capibaribe and the Mississippi rivers. Use these ideas as building blocks for your own grooves based on this sticking pattern. These patterns are all played at 90 bpm.

Example 1
With a New Orleans Swing feel

 **TRACK 75**

Example 2

 **TRACK 76**

Now let's move the right hand to a mounted cowbell on the bass drum and keep the left hand on the snare drum. This gives the maracatu groove a strong Mardi Gras Indian tinge. Try playing these grooves in between the New Orleans and Brazilian swing feel.

Example 3 – Brazilian Swing feel

TRACK 77
0:00–0:14

Example 4 – Brazilian Swing feel

TRACK 77
0:15–0:30

Now let's add some melody to these grooves by using the toms.

Example 5 – New Orleans Swing feel

TRACK 78
0:00–0:14

Example 6 – Straight 8th feel

TRACK 78
0:16–0:30

Example 7 – New Orleans Swing feel

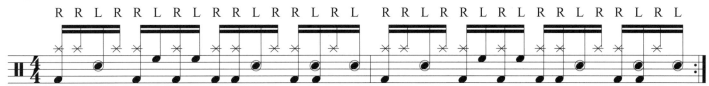

Example 8 – New Orleans Swing feel

Example 9

Example 10

Maracatu Drum & Bass (140 bpm)
Example 11

Example 12

Example 13 – Brazilian Swing feel

TRACK 80
0:00–0:13

Example 14 – Straight 8th feel

TRACK 80
0:14–0:28

Example 15

Example 16

Example 17 – Straight 8th feel

 TRACK 81

Example 18

Example 19

Example 20

Example 21

Example 22

Example 23

Example 24

Try playing the alfaia part for Baque de Marcação in the hands using the RRLR–RLRL sticking pattern and a Second Line groove bass drum.

Example 25 – Brazilian Swing feel

 TRACK 82

New Orleans Bell Patterns with Maracatu

Here are some ideas for morphing New Orleans bell patterns with maracatu.

Example 1

Example 2

TRACK 83
0:00-0:13

Example 3

Example 4

TRACK 83
0:14-0:27

Example 5

Example 6

TRACK 84
0:00-0:13

Example 7

Example 8

TRACK 84
0:14-0:27

Example 9

Example 10

TRACK 85
0:00-0:13

Here's a Hatian bell pattern called the cinquillo that is also played a lot by the Mardi Gras Indian groups in New Orleans. This works really well with maracatu.

Example 11

Example 12

TRACK 85
0:14-0:27

Example 13

Example 14

TRACK 86

Example 15

Example 16

James Black—"Hook & Sling" Morphed into a Maracatu

Here's an outline of the groove that James Black played on Eddie Bo's "Hook & Sling."

We can morph James' groove from "Hook & Sling" into a maracatu by changing only the bass drum.

Now let's take this groove and add a linear hi-hat pattern to it.

In this variation we'll only make a slight change on the last snare hit by displacing it by one sixteenth note. This is the groove I played on Nation Beat's version of "Hook & Sling."

New Orleans Mambo + Maracatu

LLRL–RLRL–RRLR–RLRR

These are some grooves I developed after exchanging some ideas with my good friend Stanton Moore. These grooves are based on the New Orleans Mambo; however, we're going to morph it into a maracatu by changing up the bass drum and playing the gonguê on the hi-hat. You should also experiment with the swing feel and try playing with a Brazilian lilt. Play the following examples with the snares off and a side stick in the left hand.

TRACK 89
0:00–0:12

TRACK 89
0:14–0:27

Now place your left hand on a mounted cowbell, and keep your right hand on the snare drum with the snares turned off.

TRACK 90

Now let's move our left hand to the hi-hat and put our right hand on a mounted cowbell. I like to mount two cowbells on my bass drum and one small cowbell on my hi-hat stand so I have the freedom to play the cowbell with either hand.

TRACK 91

Keep the snares off on this one.

 TRACK 92

Zigaboo and Maracatu

RLRL–RLRL–RRLR–RLRL

Here's an example of Zigaboo Modeliste's original groove on The Meters' "Hey Pocky A-Way."

Now let's superimpose a maracatu caixa pattern from the Baque de Imalê groove on top of Zigaboo's bass drum groove. Experiment going in between a New Orleans swing feel and a Brazilian maracatu feel. The first time through is played with a New Orleans feel, and the second time through with a Brazilian feel.

 **TRACK 93**
0:00-0:15

Now let's add some melody using the toms. This variation is based on Baque de Marcação.

 **TRACK 93**
0:17-0:33

Keep the same sticking pattern but now add some buzz rolls.

Buzz rolls and melody example A

Buzz rolls and melody example B

TRACK 94

This one is based on Baque de Imalê in the caixa and the alfaia.

This one works really well with a New Orleans swing and played a little bit slower.

 **TRACK 95**

Now let's try the same groove with a different sticking pattern. We're still morphing Zigaboo's groove into a maracatu.

RLRL–RLRL–RRLL–RRLL

Let's start off by experimenting with accents. The first example uses Zigaboo's groove in the feet while the hands are playing the Baque de Marcação alfaia part with the accents.

This example is with the Baque de Imalê alfaia part in the hands. This one works really well going in between the New Orleans and Brazilian swing feel.

This one also works really well going in between the New Orleans and Brazilian swing feel.

Now let's morph the "Hey Pocky A-Way" groove into a maracatu using the floor tom. This groove is also nice going in between the New Orleans and Brazilian swing feel.

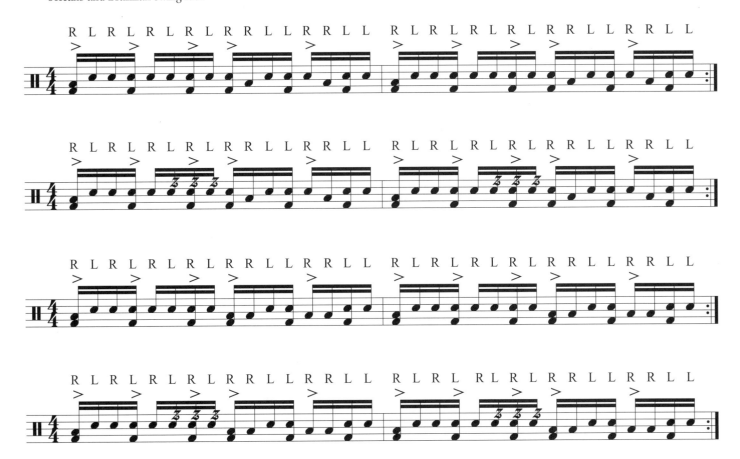

Now let's change the accents around. Here's a backbeat idea that can be a lot of fun to play on a funk tune.

TRACK 96
0:00-0:15

Continuing in the spirit of Zigaboo, let's add our left hand on the hi-hat. This gives the groove a linear vibe.

TRACK 96
0:16-0:33

TRACK 97
0:00-0:15

122

Imalê

TRACK 97
0:16-0:32

 TRACK 98

"Temos Rei, Temos Rainha" (We have Kings and Queens) performed by Maracatu New York. This is a traditional song from the community of Maracatu Nação Estrela Brilhante. On this track we play Baque de Marcação. Try playing along with this track using the material you've learned from this book.

SUGGESTED LISTENING

Here's a list of some traditional Maracatu Nations from Recife and surrounding neighborhoods who have recorded their own CD. These CDs might be hard to find but they're out there. Also search for videos of these groups on YouTube.

Maracatu Nação Estrela Brilhante

Maracatu Nação Porto Rico

Maracatu Nação Leão Coroado

Maracatu Nação Estrela Brilhante de Igarassu

Maracatu Nação Cambinda Estrela

Maracatu Nação Encanto da Alegria

Maracatu Nação Elefante

Maracatu Nação Aurora Africana

Maracatu Nação Raízes de Pai Adão

Maracatu Nação Leão da Campina

Here are some contemporary groups and artists who use maracatu a lot as a foundation in their music.

Nation Beat	DJ Dolores
Maracatu New York	Hermeto Pascoal
Chico Science & Nação Zumbi	Egberto Gismonte
Mestre Ambrosio	Naná Vasconcelos
Orquestra Popular da Bomba do Hemeterio	Cyro Baptista & Beat the Donkey
Renata Rosa	Quarteto Olinda
Mestre Salustiano	Siba
Alceu Valença	Silvério Pessoa
Antonio Carlos Nóbrega	Lenine
Cascabulho	Orquestra Contemporânea de Olinda
Chão e Chinelo	Tiné
Maciel Salu	DJ Tudo

BiBLiOGRAPHY

Andrade, Mário de. *Danças dramáticas do Brasil*. Oneida Alvarenga (org.) Belo Horizonte: Itatiaia; Brasília: INL/Pró-Memória, 1982, Tomo I.

_____. A calunga dos maracatus. In *Antologia do Carnaval do Recife*. Silva, Leonardo Dantas; Maior, Mário Souto (org.) Recife: Massangana/Fundaj, 1991.

Bastos, Daniela. *Maracatu Leão Coroado—140 anos*. Monografia (Especialização em Etnomusicologia) – Departamento de Música, Centro de Artes e Comunicação, Universidade Federal de Pernambuco, Recife, 2005.

Barbosa, Virginia. *A reconstrução musical e sócio-religiosa do maracatu nação Estrela Brilhante (Recife): Casa Amarela / Alto José do Pinho (1993–2001)*. Monografia de conclusão de especialização em Etnomusicologia, UFPE, 2001.

Benjamin, Roberto Emerson Câmara. *Folguedos e Danças de Pernambuco*. Recife: Fundação de Cultura Cidade do Recife, 1989.

Castro, Josué de. *Geography of Hunger*. Rio de Janeiro: O Cruzeiro, 1946.

Conner, Ron. *Brazilian Blackface: Maracatu Cearense and the Politics of Participation*. Paper presented at the 54 Annual Meeting of the Society for Ethnomusicology November 19, 2009 http://ucla.academia.edu/RonConner/Papers/260580/Brazilian_Blackface_Maracatu_Cearense_and_the_Politics_of_Participation

Crook, Larry. *Brazilian Music Northeastern Traditions and the Heartbeat of a Modern Nation*.Santa Barbara, California: ABC-CLIO, 2005.

_____. *Focus: Music of Northeast Brazil*. New York: Routledge, 2009.

Galinsky, Philip. *Maracatu Atômico*. New York and London: Routledge, 2002.

García Canclini. *Hybrid Cultures*. Minneapolis: University of Minnesota Press, 1990.

Guerra-Peixe, César. *Maracatus do Recife*. Recife: Fundação de Cultura, 1981.

Lima, Ivaldo Marciano de França. *Maracatus-Nação. Ressignificando Velhas Histórias*. Recife:Bagaço, 2005.

_____; Guillen, Isabel Cristina Martins. *Cultura Afro-Descendente no Recife: Maracatus, Valentes e Catimbós*. Recife: Bagaço, 2007.

_____. *Maracatu e Maracatuzeiros: Desconstruindo Certeza, Batendo Afayas e Fazendo Histórias, 1930–1945*. Recife: Edições Bagaço, 2008.

_____. *Identidade Negra no Recife: Maracatus e Afoxés*. Recife:Edições Bagaço, 2009.

Matta, Roberto. *Carnavais, Malandros e Heróis*. Rio de Janeiro: Zahar, 1980.

Maior, Mário Souto; Silva, Leonardo Dantas. *Antologia do Carnaval do Recife*. Recife: Massangana, 1991.

Perrone, Charles. *Brazilian Popular Music & Globalization*. Gainesville: University Press of Florida, c2001.

Real, Katarina. *O Folclore no Carnaval do Recife*. Recife: Massangana, 1990.

_____. *Eudes, o Rei do Maracatu*. Recife: Massangana, 2001.

Sandroni, Carlos. *O Destino de Joventina*. In: Música & Cultura. Revista Online de Etnomusicologia. Número 2, 2007. http://www .musicaecultura.ufba.br/numero_02/artigo_sandroni_01.htm

Silva, Ana Cláudia Rodrigues da. *"Vamos Maracatucá!!!" Um Estudo sobre os Maracatus Cearenses.* Master's thesis, Universidade Federal de Pernambuco, 2004. http://www.antropologia.com.br/divu/colab/d29-asilva.pdf

Silva, Leonardo Dantas (Org.). *Alguns Documentos para a História da Escravidão*. Recife: Massangana, 1988.

_____. *A Calunga de Angola Nos Maracatus do Recife*. In *Estudos sobre a Escravidão Negra*. Recife: Massangana, 1988.

Telles, José. *Do Frevo ao MangueBeat*. São Paulo: Editora 34, 2000.

Kolinski, Ana Beatriz Zanine. *Nas fronteiras entre mito e história: o caso da nação do maracatu Porto Rico*. Paper presented at the X Encontro Nacional de História Oral. Universidade Federal de Pernambuco. April 26–April 30, 2010, Rico. http://www .encontro2010.historiaoral.org.br/resources/anais/2/1270577211_ARQUIVO_NasFronteirasEntreMitoeHistoria.pdf

PRONUNCIATION GUIDE

Note: This pronunciation glossary in an approximate representation of the sounds of the words and is not an accurate phonetic transcription.

Afoxé (ah-foh-SHEH): Rhythm and dance associated with Candomblé. It is also the denomination for groups that play this specific rhythm in Bahia, Pernambuco, and other states in Brazil.

Agbê (ah-BEH)

Apito (ah-PEE-too)

Atabaque (ah-tah-BAH-kee)

Babalorixá (ba-ba-loh-ree-SHA): A priest and leader of an Afro-religion group in Brazil.

Biancó (bee-an-KAW)

Caixa (KA-ee-sha)

Calunga (kah-LOON-gah): A doll carried by the "dama-de-paço" in a Maracatu de Baque Virado group. It is also an important religious figure in the traditional Maracatu groups.

Candomblé (kahn-dohn-BLEH): Afro-Brazilian religion with Catholic influences.

Dama-de-Paço (DAH-mah dee PAH-soo): The character in a traditional maracatu group that carries the calunga doll.

Eguns (eh-GOON-sh): Spirits of dead ancestors.

Gonguê (gon-GEH)

Ijexá (ee-zheh-SHAH): Rhythm played in the afoxés.

Jurema (zhoo-REH-ma): Afro-Indigenous religion from the northeast of Brazil.

Macaíba (ma-kah-EE-bah): Type of wood used to make the alfaias from an endangered tree trunk.

Mangue (MAHN-gee): mangrove; swamp. The name of a musical movement originated in the early '90s in Recife, capital of Pernambuco.

Maracatu de Baque Virado (ma-ra-ka-TOO dee BAH-kee vee-RAH-doo)

Maracatuzeiro (mah-rah-kah-tu-ZEH-ee-roo): A member of a Maracatu de Baque Virado nation.

Melê (meh-LEH)

Mestre (MEHSH-tree)

Mineiro (mee-NEH-ee-roo)

Nação (na-SOW): Nation; a traditional group of Maracatu de Baque Virado.

Nações (nah-SOW-eesh)

Orixás (oh-ree-SHASH): Gods (and Goddesses) the deities worshipped in the Candomblé religion.

Parafolclórico (pah-rah-fohw-KLO-ree-koo): Non-folkloric groups that present dances and rhythms originated from traditional folkloric groups.

Tarol (ta-ROH-oo)

Yalorixá (ee-ah-loh-ree-SHAH): A priestess and leader of an Afro-religious group in Brazil.

Yandarrum (ee-an-dah-HOON)

HAL LEONARD PRESENTS
FAKE BOOKS FOR BEGINNERS!

Entry-level fake books! These books feature larger-than-most fake book notation with simplified harmonies and melodies – and all songs are in the key of C. An introduction addresses basic instruction in playing from a fake book.

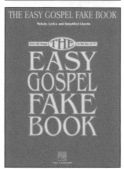

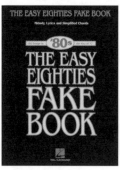
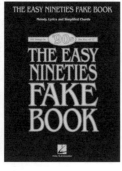

YOUR FIRST FAKE BOOK
00240112...$19.95

THE EASY FAKE BOOK
00240144...$19.95

THE SIMPLIFIED FAKE BOOK
00240168...$19.95

THE BEATLES EASY FAKE BOOK
00240309...$25.00

THE EASY BROADWAY FAKE BOOK
00240180...$19.95

THE EASY CHILDREN'S FAKE BOOK
00240428 ....$19.99

THE EASY CHRISTIAN FAKE BOOK
00240328...$19.99

THE EASY CHRISTMAS FAKE BOOK – 2ND EDITION
00240209...$19.95

THE EASY CLASSIC ROCK FAKE BOOK
00240389 ....$19.99

THE EASY CLASSICAL FAKE BOOK
00240262...$19.95

THE EASY COUNTRY FAKE BOOK
00240319...$19.95

THE EASY DISNEY FAKE BOOK
00240551...$19.99

THE EASY EARLY SONGS FAKE BOOK
00240337 ....$19.99

THE EASY FOLKSONG FAKE BOOK
00240360...$19.99

THE EASY GOSPEL FAKE BOOK
00240169...$19.95

THE EASY HYMN FAKE BOOK
00240207...$19.95

THE EASY JAZZ STANDARDS FAKE BOOK
00102346...$19.99

THE EASY LATIN FAKE BOOK
00240333...$19.99

THE EASY MOVIE FAKE BOOK
00240295...$19.95

THE EASY SHOW TUNES FAKE BOOK
00240297...$19.95

THE EASY STANDARDS FAKE BOOK
00240294...$19.95

THE EASY 3-CHORD FAKE BOOK
00240388 ....$19.99

THE EASY WORSHIP FAKE BOOK
00240265...$19.95

MORE OF THE EASY WORSHIP FAKE BOOK
00240362 ....$19.99

THE EASY TWENTIES FAKE BOOK
00240336 ....$19.99

THE EASY THIRTIES FAKE BOOK
00240335 ....$19.99

THE EASY FORTIES FAKE BOOK
00240252...$19.95

MORE OF THE EASY FORTIES FAKE BOOK
00240287...$19.95

THE EASY FIFTIES FAKE BOOK
00240255...$19.95

MORE OF THE EASY FIFTIES FAKE BOOK
00240288...$19.95

THE EASY SIXTIES FAKE BOOK
00240253...$19.95

MORE OF THE EASY SIXTIES FAKE BOOK
00240289...$19.95

THE EASY SEVENTIES FAKE BOOK
00240256...$19.95

MORE OF THE EASY SEVENTIES FAKE BOOK
00240290...$19.95

THE EASY EIGHTIES FAKE BOOK
00240340 ....$19.99

THE EASY NINETIES FAKE BOOK
00240341 ....$19.99

FOR MORE INFORMATION, SEE YOUR LOCAL MUSIC DEALER,
OR WRITE TO:

HAL•LEONARD®
CORPORATION
7777 W. BLUEMOUND RD. P.O. BOX 13819 MILWAUKEE, WI 53213

www.halleonard.com

0313

Prices, contents and availability subject to change without notice.